Modern world issues

T4-ALB-100

Series editor: John Turner

human rights

DAVID SELBY

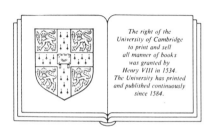

The right of the
University of Cambridge
to print and sell
all manner of books
was granted by
Henry VIII in 1534.
The University has printed
and published continuously
since 1584.

Cambridge University Press
Cambridge
London   New York   New Rochelle
Melbourne   Sydney

Published by the Press Syndicate of the University of Cambridge
The Pitt Building, Trumpington Street, Cambridge CB2 1RP
32 East 57th Street, New York, NY 10022, USA
10 Stamford Road, Oakleigh, Melbourne 3166, Australia

© Cambridge University Press 1987

First published 1987

Printed in Great Britain at the University Press, Cambridge

British Library cataloguing in publication data
Selby, David
Human rights. – (Modern world issues)
1. Civil rights
I. Title II. Series
323.4JC571

Library of Congress cataloguing card number: 87 – 14795

ISBN 0 521 27419 2

Acknowledgements

Line drawings by John Blackman; maps by Oxford Illustrators; illustration p. 25 by Beryl Sanders.
The author and publisher would like to thank the following for permission to reproduce illustrations:
p.6 Nigel Luckhurst; p.7 (above) BBC Hulton Picture Library; p.7 (below) International Defence & Aid Fund for Southern Africa; p.12 (above) Crown Copyright, reproduced with permission of the Controller of Her Majesty's Stationery Office; p. 12 (below) The Travellers Video Project; p.13 (left) United Nations; p.13 (below) Conscience Canada Inc; p.14 (left) Women's Reproductive Rights Information Centre, 52–4 Featherstone St, London EC1Y 8RT; p.14 (right) Life, 118–120 Warwick St, Leamington Spa, Warwickshire CV32 4QY, England (readers may send a large stamped addressed envelope for leaflets etc. for project work); p.15 (above) The National Anti-Vivisection Society; p.16 The Photo Source; p.17 United Nations (UN 94 896); p.18 Barnaby's Picture Library; p.20 (above and below) UPI/Bettmann Newsphotos; p.21 Shelter; p.23 Avni Ayyildiz; p.24 map based on the Peters projection, reproduced courtesy of Dr Arno Peters; p.26 United Society for the Propagation of the Gospel; p.27 Peter Brooks; p.29 Amnesty International; p.30 © Mogens Norgaard/Amnesty International; p.31 Jose Lavanderos Yanez; p.33 (above) © 1986 MacNelly, Tribune Media Services; p.33 (below) F. Rowsell, Camera Press Ltd; p.34 © 1986 Auth. Universal Press Syndicate; p.35, p.37 (above) Amnesty International; p.37 (below) © P. Reddaway/Amnesty International; p.39 Society for Cultural Relations with the USSR; p.40 © Chris McLeod; p.42, 43 (above and below) TAPOL, British Campaign for the Defence of Political Prisoners and Human Rights in Indonesia, 8a Treport St, London SW18 2BP; p.45 New Statesman; p.47 (above, middle, below) Terje Brantenberg; p.48 Toralf Sandaker; p.49 The Australian Information Service, London; p.50 © 1977 Ron Cobb, all rights reserved, used with permission of Wild and Woolley; p.51 The Teacher 4/11/83; p.53 © Hector Breeze, p.56 Equal Opportunities Commission; p.57 Theo van Boven; p.59 New Internationalist; p.61 European Court; p.62 The Scotsman Publications Ltd; p.66, 67, 68 Amnesty International; p.69 The Anti-slavery Society for the Protection of Human Rights; p.70 (above) Survival International for the Rights of Threatened Tribal Peoples, 29 Craven St, London WC2N 2NT; p.70 (below) Minority Rights Group; p.71 (above) Campaign Against Arms Trade; p.71 (middle) Stefan Verwey; p.71 (below) British Council of Churches; p.72 Writers and Scholars Educational Trust, 39c Highbury Place, London N5 1QP; p.73 (above) Humanitas International Human Rights Committee; p.73 (middle and below) Australian Human Rights Commission; p.75 (above and below) Tools for Self-Reliance, Netley Marsh Workshops, Southampton SO4 2GY; p.76 Oxfam.

Every effort has been made to reach copyright holders; the publishers would be glad to hear from anyone whose rights they have unknowingly infringed.

cover illustration: 'You must have a fair chance for a safe and healthy life, and the chance to improve your life by having a decent home, good food, an education, employment and access to enjoyment through music, arts, sport and other hobbies and activities' (*Universal Declaration of Human Rights*). Photograph by Adrian Rowland.

Contents

LIBRARY
ALMA COLLEGE
ALMA, MICHIGAN

To Bärbel, Rowena and Jan

Thanks also to Shirley Brewer, formerly of the Centre for Global Education, University of York, who typed the manuscript; David Dunetz, Centre for Global Education, who kindly contributed material; and Bärbel who gave me so much support.

1   What are human rights?

Mother Distraught Over Discoloured Baby

Leicester Echo 29 Dec 2006

CHRISTMAS was a distressing time for Anne and Roger Benson of Station Road, Leicester, when Anne gave birth to a discoloured baby daughter. The child was immediately sent to a maternity hospital in Outland Area 4 (Wales), accompanied by an outland wet-nurse. This was the fourteenth case of hereditary mishap in Leicester in the last month. Anne and Roger, both respected members of the community, have no other children.

Divorce Rate Success

Dec. 2006 Central Britain News

The Marriage Annulment Committee for the Eastern Region of Central Britain reports that the simplified annulment procedures introduced by the Government in August have enabled the Committee to treble the number of cases dealt with each month. It now estimates that the backlog of Eastern Section cases involving marriages between blue-eyeds and discoloureds dating from pre-Separation days will be cleared by 2011.

Terrorist Arrested

O.C. 16 Jan '07

James McCarthy, unemployed resident of Outland Area 6 (Scotland) was taken into custody yesterday after police searched his home and discovered an exercise book of poetry containing anti-Separationist sentiments. He will appear before Area 6 Judge Herbert Simmons tomorrow. The maximum penalty is a life sentence to one of the Hebridean island labour camps.

Job Vacancies In Central Britain

Outlands Chronicle 18 May '06

Discoloured male personnel wishing to obtain work in the industrial cities of Central Britain are asked to report to their local employment bureau before 31 May. Vacancies exist in Birmingham, Leicester, Manchester, Southampton and London. Applicants are reminded that in keeping with the Temporary Labour Law, 24 September 2005, employment of discoloureds in Central Britain is for a fixed term of one year, renewable on good report. Temporary workers are also reminded that they face imprisonment if they fail to produce a current work permit on demand. Travel between Central Britain and the outland areas during the permit period is forbidden.

***

Clearance Now Complete

Central Brit. News 16 May '06

DISCOLOUREDS EVACUATED
The evacuation of brown-eyeds, green-eyeds and grey-eyeds from Central Britain is at last complete. Six trains left Liverpool Lime Street Station between 9 a.m. and 10 a.m. yesterday, carrying the remaining resident discoloureds in Central Britain to outland areas. Their presence in Central Britain is now restricted to males for whom temporary work is available in industrial centres and to females in hospitals, factories and restaurants.

and inspection service.

* * * * * * * * * * * * * * * *

Julie McCarthy, wife of political poet, Jim McCarthy, was battered to death by prison warders yesterday. Jim, arrested last week for writting anti-Separationist poetry refused to give the names of fellow Anti-Separationists, even under electric shock treatment. The warders then tried to break Jim by beating up his wife while he looked on chained and helpless. Julie died a few hours later from her injuries. *Outland Underground 21 Jan 2007*

What you have just read are six fictional newspaper extracts giving glimpses of life in a society very different from Britain today. In each extract freedoms which many of us take for granted have been taken

5

away from people because of the colour of their eyes. Imaginary though this society is, each of the incidents described is based upon events that have actually taken place in the last few years. The mass resettlement of people against their will has been a feature of the recent history of, for example, Kampuchea. In 1975 the government instituted a harsh regime, forcibly evacuating all towns and cities, and setting the population to work in the fields. In South Africa there are various forms of population control and blacks in certain 'homeland' areas need permits to work in cities; until 1986 an 'Immorality Act' forbade marriage between whites and 'non-whites'; the mass resettlement of people against their will has long been South African policy (since the late nineteenth century). The arrest, imprisonment and unfair trial of people for their political beliefs is commonplace in many parts of the world as is the use of torture, including the torture of friends and relatives of those held by the authorities. All over the world human rights and freedoms are daily denied to people because of their gender, race, colour, national origin, class, age, religious beliefs or political opinions.

Legal, moral and human rights

What are rights? One way to answer the question is to think of some of the ways in which the word is used in the English language. When someone says 'I know my rights', or 'We're within our rights', they are claiming or recognising that in fairness and justice they are entitled to have or do certain things. A right is something to which we are entitled.

When we claim our rights we often base our claim upon the law of the land. As we mature towards adulthood, our rights as guaranteed by the law grow in number. In Britain, for example, the child is given the right to go to school at five; at twelve the child obtains the right to buy pet animals; at sixteen the right to ride a motorbike, leave school and begin full-time work; at eighteen the individual gains the right to marry without parental consent. Rights that are laid down in law are called *legal* rights. Legal rights are in a sense the most solid of all rights in that they can be defended in a national court of law. A citizen denied what she or he considers to be a legal right can seek redress through the courts.

Most but not all legal rights are written down. Many countries (for example Canada, West Germany, the United States and the Soviet Union) have a written constitution, basic law or bill of rights describing what citizens have the right to do or expect. British law works the other way

We hold these truths to be self-evident, that all men are created equal, that they are endowed by their Creator with certain inalienable rights, that among these are life, liberty and the pursuit of happiness.
The American Declaration of Independence, 4 July 1776

THIS IS A
PRIVATE RIGHT OF WAY
AND MUST BE KEPT
FREE OF OBSTRUCTION
AT ALL TIMES

round. There is no such thing as a basic law guaranteeing people's rights. It is assumed that people have the right to do something unless a law has been made by parliament expressly forbidding it.

Legal rights are not, however, the whole story. People also base their claim to rights on *general principles* of fairness and justice. For example, the mother of a family might complain, 'I have the right to be consulted about what is going on in my home.' In this case, she is not basing her claim on actual state law as there is no law saying that mothers must be consulted by their families. She is appealing to the principle that parents are entitled to be consulted when family decisions affecting their home are made. Rights arising out of such general principles of fairness and justice are called *moral* rights.

It is helpful, perhaps, to think of legal rights as being concerned with *fact* and of moral rights as being *aspirations* or *ideals*. A moral right may or may not be enforced and supported by the law of the land.

In claiming a moral right, people employ all sorts of justifications in support of their case. Sometimes they imply that they have *earned* a moral right because of the role they perform or position they occupy in society. Teachers claim the right to offer advice to young people about their academic and moral development and about their choice of career. They also claim the right to discipline their pupils. Pupils, for their part, are increasingly demanding a say in deciding school policy since that policy affects them directly (see Chapter 11). The mother in the example given earlier is claiming the right to be consulted about what is going on in the home because of her position as parent. Sometimes people claim certain rights because of what they earn through their work (by writing a book an author may gain both a *moral* and *legal* right to a percentage of the proceeds from sales). The important thing to note about some of the moral rights so far discussed is that they are claimed *by people in particular situations*. They are not rights that can be claimed by all peoples in all situations. What the law lays down can, of course, conflict with what people see as their moral right. In the imaginary society with which this chapter begins, the law discriminated against people of certain eye colours and, by so doing, violated the moral rights of citizens in a number of ways. To cause families to be broken up, for example, as happens in South Africa under

Suffragettes demonstrating in London, 1912. British women campaigning for the vote claimed that they had the *moral right* to vote. When in 1918 parliament granted the vote to certain women over the age of thirty, this right became both a *legal* and a *moral* one.

South African pass laws document: under the pass laws system, the movement of the black African majority was tightly controlled. Even though the laws were abolished in 1986, there are still severe restrictions on freedom of movement.

The system of Apartheid in South Africa, under which a black African majority of 25 million is dominated by a white minority of 5 million and denied the basic freedoms and benefits of the country's great wealth is a present-day example of an entire legal system flying in the face of moral right. Internal and international pressure is now forcing some changes in South Africa.

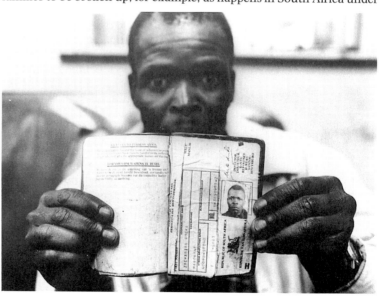

the pass law system, is an offence against general justice regardless of whether such policies have the backing of the law and the state. Yet there is a flip side to that coin: taking a child into care breaks up a family and violates the rights of parents, but it is both legally and morally right to do so if a child's life is at risk. Thinking about rights will almost always involve some kind of clash between different kinds of rights – there are few cut and dried answers.

There is a further and higher category of moral rights and that is rights which apply to all people at all times in all situations. We call such rights *human rights*. By definition, human rights are not earned, bought or inherited. Nor do they 'go with the job'. Human rights are possessed by everybody in the world because they are human. People are equally entitled to them regardless of their gender, race, colour, language, national origin, age, class or religious or political creed.

Human rights are universal in a further respect, too. Not only do we all equally possess them; we all have *duties* imposed upon us by them. If we say that all humans are in equal possession of certain rights, then what we are in fact saying is that we have a duty to recognise, respect and uphold the rights of our fellow human beings. Perhaps the easiest way to understand this idea is to think of what life would be like for you if people failed to respect your rights. What would a typical day be like if everybody you met failed to respect your freedom to speak, your freedom to own property, your right to privacy, your right to a safe and healthy environment, your freedom from degrading treatment and punishment? Only when others fulfil their duties to you as a human being are you able to enjoy your rights. Equally, only when you meet your obligations to them can they enjoy theirs. The duties imposed on people by human rights are universal and in no way limited to specific persons or groups or to the citizens of one state.

Some human rights are more important or *basic* than others. The right to life is the most basic of all for without it all other rights are in jeopardy. Freedom of speech or the right to rest and leisure, for instance, count for very little if our right to life is not guaranteed. Amongst other *basic human rights* are the right to be recognised as a person before the law, the right to equal protection in law and freedom from arbitrary arrest and detention. Basic human rights provide the foundation upon which the enjoyment of other human rights depends. They are also rights which cannot be restricted or taken away without affront to human dignity and which any society has a fundamental duty to protect at all times. Later on in this chapter it is suggested that the full exercise of many of our rights is restricted in practice because we would otherwise violate the rights of others. This is not the case with basic human rights. Our right to be recognised as a person before the law, for example, is not limited by the rights of other people; a society which fails to acknowledge that right can justifiably be criticised.

Another model for looking at human rights

There are real problems, however, in identifying what our basic human rights are and in deciding where they end and where other types of human rights begin. We would probably want to add to our cluster of basic human rights the right to physical well-being, to security, to some liberty and some property, for it would clearly be the case that our human dignity would be undermined were we denied

Legal rights are rights laid down in law.
Moral rights are rights based on general principles of fairness and justice. They may be particular or universal.
Human rights are universal moral rights: they belong to everybody because they are human.

You can think of **liberty-oriented rights** as rights that promote individual freedom. You can think of **security-oriented rights** as those rights that give the individual social and economic security. Each set of rights complements the other: for example, freedom of speech helps us to claim the right to a good health service; the security that a good health service provides enables people to be more vigorous in demanding and defending their liberty-oriented rights.

Different types of rights, shown in diagram form (based on the *Universal Declaration of Human Rights*).

these things. The difficulty here is that we have to draw from the two other major categories of human rights – liberty-oriented rights and security-oriented rights – if we are to put flesh on what we mean. *Liberty-oriented rights* are rights concerned with giving individuals freedom of action and choice, and freedom to participate in the political life of their community and society. *Security-oriented rights* seek to protect people's physical, material, social and economic well-being. In the final analysis, there is a grey area between basic human rights on the one hand and liberty- and security-oriented rights on the other in that, whatever one's political viewpoint, our essential humanity would be undermined if we were not in every circumstance given some liberty and some security. A certain – admittedly imprecise – level of liberty and security must therefore form part of a working definition of basic human rights. Liberty-oriented rights (sometimes called *civil and political rights*) and security-oriented rights (sometimes referred to as *economic, social and cultural rights*) not only differ in what they are seeking to protect but also in their quality as rights. In the first place, they carry very different implications for governments. Liberty-oriented rights aim to give individuals as much freedom and control over their own lives as possible. They therefore provide defences for the individual against excessive state power by limiting what governments and government bodies can do. Governments cannot, for example, open people's letters, prevent people publishing things, stop people worshipping in church or prevent travelling, unless they can show that they have good reason for doing so. Most security-oriented rights, on the other hand, require significant levels of government involvement and intervention if they are to be achieved. Free education of good quality for all citizens is not likely to be secured – or maintained – unless the government supplies the funds and operates an advisory and inspection service for schools. The right to

4 Within the cluster of human rights are a nucleus of **basic human rights**. Basic human rights cannot be taken away without affronting human dignity. They must, therefore, include some liberty and some security.

There may be a clash between legal rights and basic human rights (e.g. in a country which legalises the death penalty for 'non-serious' crimes).

3 Human rights are usually divided into **liberty-oriented rights** and **security-oriented rights**.

There are more liberty-oriented rights than security-oriented rights enshrined in law, because it is easier to ensure the right to freedom, for example, than the right to social security, especially in a poor country.

2 Human rights are universal moral rights (e.g. freedom from torture).

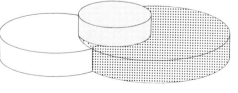

Sometimes human rights are also enshrined in law (e.g. freedom of speech in Britain).

1 We have **moral rights** and **legal rights** (rights enshrined in law). We have more moral than legal rights.

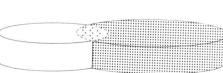

Sometimes moral and legal rights overlap i.e. when a moral right is enshrined in law (e.g. a woman's right to vote in the USA, for instance, is a moral and legal one).

■ – basic human rights   ▤ – security-oriented rights   ▥ – liberty-oriented rights

◻ – human rights   ◻ – legal rights   ▦ – moral rights

Security-Oriented Rights
(THE RIGHT TO WELL-BEING)

EVERYONE HAS AND RIGHT TO REST AND LEISURE; YOUR WORKING DAY SHOULD NOT BE TOO LONG AND YOU ARE ENTITLED TO REGULAR HOLIDAYS WITH PAY.

YOU MUST HAVE A FAIR CHANCE FOR A SAFE AND HEALTHY LIFE, AND THE CHANCE TO IMPROVE YOUR LIFE BY HAVING A DECENT HOME, GOOD FOOD, AN EDUCATION, EMPLOYMENT, AND ACCESS TO ENJOYMENT THROUGH MUSIC, ARTS, SPORT AND OTHER HOBBIES AND ACTIVITIES

(EQUAL PAY FOR EQUAL WORK)

WE ALL HAVE THE RIGHT TO WORK AND TO CHOOSE OUR KIND OF WORK

THE RIGHT TO FORM OR JOIN A TRADE UNION TO PROTECT YOUR INTRESTS AT WORK

THE RIGHT TO REASONABLE PAYMENT FOR WORK DONE (ENOUGH TO SUPPORT YOU AND YOUR FAMILY). THE RIGHT TO WELFARE PAYMENTS IF YOUR WAGE IS INADEQUATE

THE RIGHT, AS A PARENT, TO CHOOSE HOW YOUR CHILDREN AND WHAT THEY WILL BE TAUGHT

The Right to Learn and go to school Paying fees.

EVERYONE HAS THE RIGHT TO A CLEAN ENVIRON.

There must be fairness in the place of work. Good working conditions & protection against unemployment

THE RIGHT TO JOIN IN THE CULTURAL LIFE OF THE COMMUNITY, ART, MUSIC, SPORT, THEATRE, ETC.

The right to be helped if you cannot work because of unemployment, illness, age or any other reason beyond your control.

THE RIGHT TO BENEFIT FROM SCIENTIFIC INVENTIONS & DISCOVERIES; COMPUTERS, MEDICINES, ETC.

ALL RIGHTS ON THIS BILLBOARD BELONG TO EVERYBODY REGARDLESS OF RACE, SEX, COLOUR, LANGUAGE, RELIGIOUS OR POLITICAL CREED, NATIONAL OR SOCIAL ORIGIN, PROPERTY, BIRTH, ETC....

Liberty-Oriented Rights
(THE RIGHTS TO FREEDOM, CHOICE AND PARTICIPATION)

The right to receive and communicate information and ideas through books, newspapers, radio, television, etc...

THE RIGHT TO THINK WHAT YOU WANT & SAY WHAT YOU LIKE

The Law must be the same for everyone; there must be no favourites before the Law

(NOBODY SHALL BE A SLAVE)

THE RIGHT TO LIFE, FREEDOM AND SAFETY

THE RIGHT TO GO TO A COURT TO SEEK JUSTICE IF THE LAW OF THE COUNTRY HAS NOT BEEN RESPECTED

FREEDOM FROM UNFAIR IMPRISONMENT OR UNFAIR EXPULSION FROM YOUR COUNTRY

THE RIGHT TO BE CONSIDERED INNOCENT UNTIL PROVED GUILTY IN A PUBLIC TRIAL

THE RIGHT TO A FAIR AND PUBLIC TRIAL IF ACCUSED OF A CRIME

The right to come and go as you wish within your country, and the right to leave and return to your country

FREEDOM FROM TORTURE AND CRUEL, DEGRADING PUNISHMENT

FREEDOM FROM INTERFERENCE IN YOUR PRIVACY, FAMILY, HOME AND CORRESPONDENCE, UNLESS THERE IS A GOOD REASON FOR PROTECTION.

IF SOMEONE HURTS OR THREATENS YOU, YOU HAVE THE RIGHT TO GO TO ANOTHER COUNTRY AND ASK FOR PROTECTION. THAT RIGHT MAY BE LOST IF YOU HAVE COMMITTED A NON-POLITICAL CRIME OR HAVE VIOLATED OTHER PEOPLE'S RIGHTS.

THE RIGHT TO MARRY WHO YOU CHOOSE. NOBODY SHALL BE FORCED TO MARRY AGAINST THEIR WILL

freedom from saying you things

The right to belong to a country and the right to keep or change your nationality unless there are good reasons against it.

The right to think for yourself, choose your own religion, the right to practise & teach that religion privately & in public

Laws everywhere must treat everyone as a person

NOBODY CAN FORCE A PERSON TO JOIN AN ORGANISATION BUT EVERYONE HAS THE RIGHT TO ARRANGE AND ATTEND PEACEFUL MEETINGS AND TO SET UP OR JOIN PEACEFUL ORGANISATIONS

THE RIGHT TO TAKE PART IN YOUR COUNTRY'S AFFAIRS BY: BELONGING TO THE GOVERNMENT IF ELECTED, CHOOSING POLITICIANS WHO HAVE IDEAS YOU SUPPORT, THROUGH FREE AND REGULAR ELECTIONS

YOU HAVE THE RIGHT TO OWN OR SHARE OWNERSHIP OF PROPERTY. YOU CANNOT BE DEPRIVED OF WHAT YOU OWN WITHOUT GOOD REASON

welfare payments for the ill, aged or unemployed demands that the government collects and distributes welfare funds (national insurance, pensions and social security). Hence, whilst liberty-oriented rights tend to limit the scope of government activity, the achievement of security-oriented rights requires government intervention and leads to greater interference in the lives of individuals.

Secondly, security-oriented rights are in most cases less easy to convert into legal rights. There are relatively few financial or practical obstacles if a government wishes to pass and implement a law guaranteeing, say, freedom of assembly or freedom from *censorship*. There are far more obstacles if a government wishes to implement the right to free education, to free healthcare and to *supplementary benefits*. Many countries are extremely poor and their governments are unable to raise enough wealth through taxes or other means to build the schools and hospitals required and to establish a system of welfare payments. The very scale of poverty makes their task impossible. In such circumstances, the achievement of security-oriented rights is necessarily seen as unattainable for the foreseeable future. If foreign or international factors largely account for a country's poverty, then any inability to satisfy citizens' security-oriented rights cannot in all fairness be blamed upon the government in question.

A similar point can often be made about the failure of governments in wealthy countries to satisfy their people's social and economic rights. The right to employment provides a useful illustration here. Most Western industrialised countries have high levels of unemployment. Some of that unemployment is caused by circumstances particular to each country but almost all people agree that the decline in the number of jobs has been caused by world-wide economic recession, a situation which no one country can control. For that reason, the right to employment cannot be simply viewed as a straightforward 'people versus government' issue as could, say, any failure to defend the citizens' freedom to worship.

Although liberty-oriented rights and security-oriented rights are very different in kind, many people argue that they are very closely linked and need to be promoted simultaneously. Security-oriented rights will not be achieved, they argue, unless people are given the political liberty to demand those rights. At the same time, people will be less vigorous in defence of their liberty-oriented rights if their economic position is desperate and their main concern is survival.

Censorship – the banning and suppression of articles, books, magazines, newspapers, films, videos, plays, television and radio programmes by the state.
Supplementary Benefit – money paid by the state to people whose total income falls below a fixed minimum.

The human rights 'billboard' *(opposite)* is based on the *Universal Declaration of Human Rights.* Many commentators on the Declaration describe it as falling into two sections – liberty-oriented, or civil and political rights (articles 1–21); and security-oriented, or economic, social and cultural rights (articles 22–8). Some of these rights, such as the right to life, freedom and safety, may be put under a further heading of 'basic human rights' (described on pages 8–9).
The sign-writer is still at work. What new rights do you think should be added?

Rights in conflict

It is one thing to decide what people's rights are, it is quite another to decide to what extent those rights can be exercised in practice. If we accept that everybody is entitled to rights simply because they are human, we straight away run into difficulties when we begin to look at examples of liberty-oriented rights in action. Let us take freedom of movement – my right to go where I want. Does that give me the right to take a short cut through somebody's garden and across their vegetable patch? Can I enter a private house without restriction? Take the example of freedom of opinion and expression – my right to say, write and publish what I want. Does that allow me to say or write offensive, vicious and untrue things about another person? In each example, the answer is no. My freedom to come and go as I wish is limited in practice

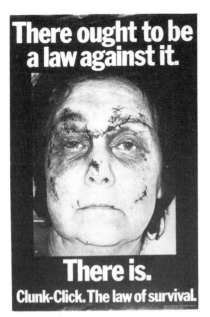

There ought to be a law against it.

There is.
Clunk-Click. The law of survival.

Are seatbelt laws a justifiable intrusion by governments into individual rights?

by the owner's right to both privacy and property. My freedom to say or write what I want is limited by the other person's right to be free of attacks upon his or her honour and reputation. The laws of slander and libel would enable the person to take me to court.

In practice the liberty-oriented rights we claim cancel each other out to a greater or lesser extent so we are never able to exercise them in an unrestricted way. A balance has to be struck between our *positive* rights (our *freedom to* do something we want) and our *negative* rights (our *freedom from* having something harmful or distasteful done to us).

The question of compulsory seatbelts illustrates this. It was only in 1983, after many years of argument, that a law came into force in Britain making the wearing of seatbelts compulsory for drivers and their front-seat passengers. Many people had opposed such a law claiming that it was an interference with people's *freedom to* decide for themselves. In the end the side won which argued that the National Health Service, hospitals, doctors and nurses should be *free from* the cost, work and worry of dealing with critically injured people who might have escaped from an accident without injury had they been wearing seatbelts. The public money (raised by taxes) and the work hours thus saved, it was also argued, could be used to better meet *the rights of others* to speedy and effective hospital treatment.

The arguments surrounding seatbelt laws raise the all-important question of whether the state has the right to interfere with the freedom of the individual in order to protect what it sees as the 'common good'. Has a water authority the right to add fluoride to our water so as to better protect our teeth and, incidentally, cut down the national dental bill? Is the consequent loss of individual choice over whether or not to drink fluoride justified? Is the government overstepping the mark when, for health and environmental reasons, it declares a densely populated urban area a 'smokeless zone'? Should people have the right to light coal fires if they wish? Suppose the government decides to build a new by-pass because of what it sees as the 'public interest' and your house stands exactly on the path of the planned route. Does the government have the right to order your eviction? Where does your right to own property stand when in conflict with the townspeople's demand that traffic congestion be reduced?

In Britain the right to own a gun is strictly limited by a licensing system. In the United States it is a simple matter to obtain a gun. The British position is that the individual right to self-defence has to be

Signs on the door of an East London pub, 1986. Britain's race laws forbid notices such as these. Discrimination is also forbidden in fields such as advertising, education and housing. Should the law interfere with the proprietor's right to decide who will enter the premises?

No Dogs Allowed

No Travellers

No Children Allowed

Pollution in the 1980s: a section of the Bogota river in Colombia; and the effects of acid rain in Scandinavia. Have those alive today the right to abuse the environment? What about the rights of future generations?

Members of Conscience Canada and the Peace Tax Campaign claim the right to have that proportion of their taxes, which is used for military purposes, diverted into a special fund. This should be used for non-military peace-making (e.g. research into resolving conflict, and cross-cultural exchanges).

Taxes for Peace NOT WAR makes sense

curtailed for reasons of public protection and safety. The US position, on the other hand, emphasises the right to self-defence. Is the British position a defensible violation of the rights of the individual?

If one's answer to some – or all – of the questions just posed is that a government does have the right to restrict individual freedom of choice and action, then further related questions follow. How do we decide where the line is to be drawn between what is a defensible and what is an indefensible restriction of our rights by government in the name of the 'common good'? Who should be involved in making that decision? Which human rights cannot be given or taken away and which ones can – in other words, what are our *basic* human rights?

Issues of individual rights versus what is seen as the greater good of the community are also raised when the state is threatened. Individual rights are often suspended by governments in time of war, revolution or other forms of public disturbance. During the Falklands War in 1982, for instance, soldiers' and sailors' letters were censored to avoid giving away military secrets. During the Second World War (1939–45) Germans living in Britain were imprisoned without trial and people were given no choice about whether or not to black out their windows at night.

There are also important areas of tension between liberty-oriented rights on the one hand and security-oriented rights on the other. As we have seen, the achievement of security-oriented rights involves active state interference in the lives of its citizens. To provide public healthcare, public education and a system of protection for the aged, infirm or unemployed is a very costly undertaking. The bulk of the money required is usually obtained through taxing income and through a tax on property (rates). The richer one is, the more one pays. Many security-oriented rights, therefore, involve the state in redistributing some of the wealth of the rich for the corporate good.

Such a redistribution of wealth inevitably conflicts with the liberty-oriented rights of the better-off. Some argue that taxation violates people's right to own property, their right to privacy and their

Since 1967,

OVER A MILLION WOMEN

HAVE HAD ABORTIONS...

... AND WE HAD OVER A

MILLION GOOD REASONS WHY

Our Bodies·Our Lives·Our Right to Decide!

Isn't this a human rights issue, too ?

Six unborn
children killed
under the
1967 Abortion Act
The youngest was about
8 weeks gestation
The oldest about 25 weeks.

Save the Unborn Child

Life

Human rights begin at conception

Abortion is a very controversial subject which raises the question of a woman's right to control her own fertility as opposed to the foetus's right to life.

(a) A pro-choice position *(above left)* means that you think every woman has the right to decide whether or not to continue her pregnancy.

(b) An anti-abortion position *(above right)* means that you think every foetus has the right to life.

right to freedom from slavery or forced labour. To take wealth from someone, they maintain, undermines their right to property; the information required to assess people's level of taxation or the rates they should pay is an intrusion into privacy and to ask people to give up a large slice of their income in the form of income tax is to ask them to work for nothing for part of every working day (which is a form of slavery).

The dilemma just touched upon raises another tension central to the field of human rights – that between freedom and equality. If we pursue equality we will almost certainly be in the business of limiting people's freedom in pursuance of a higher measure of security for the less privileged whilst if we allow the rich and powerful unlimited freedom, then levels of inequality within society will grow.

Various arguments have been put forward in explanation of why human rights are so important. One view is that the idea of human rights has been developed to identify and guarantee the most fundamental concerns and needs of humankind. Human rights are a way of defending our deepest interests as humans. Another view, not in conflict with the first, is that human rights stem from the characteristics which distinguish us from other animals – such as our capacity for reason and self-reflection, our ability to understand past, present and future and the idea of progress, our consciousness of the wider world and the fact that we have a conscience which enables us to make judgements about right and wrong. Our inherent human dignity requires that we have human rights to preserve and promote that

A 'cannula', or fine tube, has been inserted through this monkey's skull, and fluids drawn off from the brain. This device is also used to introduce drugs and other substances into the brain, for research purposes. Many animal rights campaigners would be very critical of the view that human beings have rights because they are human. They would argue that all animals have rights, human and non-human, and to single out humans is 'speciesist'. Do non-human animals have the same rights as human animals?

dignity. A third view is that we have human rights because we are conscious beings and need protection from physical and psychological pain. When our rights are violated we suffer pain. This third view differs from the first and second in that the distinction between humankind and the rest of the animal world becomes rather blurred since animals are conscious beings and also suffer pain.

Widespread consciousness of human rights and their importance is a post Second World War phenomenon. How did this come about? How are human rights interpreted, and which are given priority, in different parts of the world? How have they been violated in recent years and how are they being violated today? What has been done and is being done at international and regional levels to combat human rights violations? How can we express an active concern for human rights in our own lives? These are some of the most important questions we will be addressing in this book. In the next two chapters we will consider the international history of human rights since 1945 and investigate some of the different perspectives on rights brought to international arenas of debate. There then follow four chapters of case studies and a further four chapters on the defence of human rights. The aim of this chapter has been to give you a framework of ideas for thinking around the issues as you read on.

2 Human rights in the 'global village'

The Universal Declaration of Human Rights

Today's world is made up of a tangled and intricate web of connections between lands and peoples. It is often referred to as the 'global village'. Many of the major problems we face require international co-operation if we are to have a chance of solving them – hence the growing number of international commissions, conferences and organisations.

The Universal Declaration of Human Rights offers us early evidence of the trend towards international co-operation. Spurred on by the bloodshed and horror of the Second World War (1939–45), the nations then at war with Germany and her allies were determined to avoid any repetition of war. Hence, they set about planning the details of an international organisation, *the United Nations*, which would work towards a better and more peaceful future. A *United Nations Charter*, defining the purposes, principles, methods and structures of the new organisation, was signed by fifty nations in 1945.

The Charter reflects the fact that people were beginning to perceive a close relationship between aggression towards other nations and a lack of respect for human rights at home. Hitler's record of inhumanity towards the Jews and other minorities and his aggressive foreign policy were held to be closely linked together. For that reason, the international protection of human rights was seen as one essential pre-condition of world peace.

In the introduction to the Charter, the peoples of the United Nations were asked to 'reaffirm faith in fundamental human rights, in the dignity and worth of the human person, in the equal rights of men and

Jews in Warsaw during the Second World War.

United Nations headquarters in New York.

women and of nations large and small'. They were also asked to 'promote social progress and better standards of life in larger freedom'.

The human rights principles laid down in the Charter were of a general nature. Something more specific was needed. The task was given to the *United Nations Commission on Human Rights*. Set up under the Charter in 1945, the Commission was asked in 1946 to prepare an 'international bill of rights'. By 1947 the Commission had decided that a Universal Declaration of Human Rights was needed first, to be followed by one or more human rights treaties (covenants), which would be legally binding on the nations that signed them. The *Universal Declaration of Human Rights* was adopted by the General Assembly of the United Nations on 10 December 1948 as 'a common standard of achievement for all peoples and all nations'.

The Declaration was not legally enforceable but its influence was far reaching. Described by one writer as 'humanity's response to the Nazi death camps, the fleeing refugees, and tortured prisoners-of-war', it was the first international statement on human rights which listed rights in a systematic manner. As such, it set a standard of conduct for nations around the world. A number of the countries that gained independence in the 1950s and 1960s quoted from the Declaration in their constitutions, so that the Declaration is now part and parcel of the constitution of some thirty states. It is also quite frequently referred to in the opening paragraphs of new laws introduced by governments. Embarrassment on the part of governments found to be denying their citizens' rights has become a powerful weapon which other governments can use against them.

The International Covenants on Human Rights

It took the United Nations a further eighteen years to produce two treaties on human rights. On 16 December 1966, the *Covenant on Civil and Political Rights* and the *Covenant on Economic, Social and Cultural Rights* were voted upon and adopted by the UN General Assembly. The Universal Declaration and the two Covenants make up the *International Bill of Rights*.

The two Covenants differ from the Universal Declaration in a number of ways. They are legally binding upon states ratifying (formally approving and signing) them. They introduce a new right, the right of all peoples and nations to 'self-determination' (the right to work out their own problems and future). They also set up a machinery for the international supervision of human rights.

How is that supervision carried out? The Covenant on Civil and Political Rights provided for the setting up of a *Human Rights Committee*. This supervises the human rights performance of states which have signed the Covenant in three ways. First, it examines reports describing how the Covenant is being implemented. Second, it can consider complaints by one state against another as long as both parties have signed a special declaration recognising the right of the Committee to hear such complaints. Third, the Committee can consider complaints from individuals if they are citizens of countries that have accepted that individuals can file complaints.

The supervisory machinery set up by the Covenant on Economic, Social and Cultural Rights is less developed largely because the rights laid down are seen as targets to aim for rather than standards

Covenant on economic, social and cultural rights

Everyone has the right to:
- the enjoyment of just and favourable conditions of work
- form trade unions
- social security
- an adequate standard of living
- the enjoyment of the highest attainable standard of physical and mental health
- education
- take part in cultural life and enjoy the benefits of scientific progress

Covenant on civil and political rights

Everyone has the right to:

- life; sentence of death may be imposed only for the most serious of crimes
- liberty and security of person
- freedom of thought, conscience and religion
- equal treatment in the courts
- be presumed innocent until proven guilty
- peaceful assembly
- freedom of association including the right to form trade unions
- take part in public affairs

No one shall be subject to:

- torture
- slavery
- forced labour
- arbitrary interference with his or her privacy, family, home or correspondence

achievable straight away. Whereas those states signing the Covenant on Civil and Political Rights were expected to ensure that their citizens had or were given those rights immediately, the same could not be expected of the Covenant on Economic, Social and Cultural Rights. Most African, Asian, Caribbean and South American countries were in no position immediately to offer everyone, for instance, 'the highest attainable standard of physical and mental health'. Hence, the machinery set up to implement the Covenant is limited to a system of reporting. States signing the Covenant agree to submit reports on progress made in the field of economic, social and cultural rights.

By September 1981, sixty-six states had ratified the Covenant on Civil and Political Rights and sixty-eight states had ratified its sister Covenant. The supervisory machinery established by the two Covenants has been found to have a number of significant weaknesses (see Chapter 8). Even so, it has played an important part in raising consciousness world-wide about human rights.

Several developments have taken place outside the United Nations. In 1950 the work of the Council of Europe led to the signing of the *European Convention on Human Rights*, the first regional human rights treaty. The European Convention (see Chapter 9) served as the model for the *American Convention on Human Rights* which took effect in 1978 and for the *African Charter of Human and People's Rights* adopted in 1981. International pressure groups have also played a significant part in bringing human rights questions to the fore in international affairs (see Chapter 10).

One effect of the growth of international law in human rights is a major change in the *status of the individual*. Before 1948 the individual was subject to the laws of the nation. If those laws violated his or her rights, there was no internationally accepted code of rights which could be turned to for justice. Nor, save in rare cases, were the interests of the individual citizen taken into account in international diplomacy. Now the rights of the individual are established regardless of what the law of the land says.

Uganda gains independence in 1962. The right to self-determination was added to international law in the 1960s.

Eastern Bloc ● Western Powers Cold War ● Iron Curtain ● Détente

Germany was defeated in 1945 as the army of the Soviet Union pushed westwards through German-occupied Eastern Europe and the armies of the other allied powers (Britain, France and the USA) pushed east. Since the Second World War, the countries of Eastern Europe (Bulgaria, Czechoslovakia, East Germany, Hungary, Rumania and Poland) have remained under Soviet control and have Communist governments. Together with the Soviet Union, they are known as the **Eastern Bloc**. The **Western Powers** are the nations of Western Europe, Canada and the USA. In 1949 they set up a military alliance called NATO (the North Atlantic Treaty Organization). Most, but not all, Western European countries are in NATO. The Eastern bloc responded with its own military alliance, the Warsaw Pact, in 1955. In the late 1940s the period of **Cold War** began between the Western and Eastern bloc countries (i.e. a state of hostility involving no actual fighting). In that period the so-called **Iron Curtain** of barbed wire, watchtowers and minefields was built along the border of Eastern bloc countries sharing a frontier with Western countries. The Cold War was followed by a period of **détente** in which the two blocs tried to exist side by side with less hostility.

Helsinki and after

The 1975 Conference on Security and Co-operation in Europe, held in Helsinki, Finland, gave the world unexpected evidence of the place human rights has achieved in international relations. For some years, *Western* and *Eastern bloc* countries had been slowly moving away from the *Cold War* they had been engaged in since the late 1940s. The Helsinki Conference was called to take the process towards *détente* further. The Soviet Union was anxious to have the West recognise the territorial changes it had imposed in Eastern Europe at the close of the Second World War. The West was prepared to go along with the Soviets as long as the USSR agreed to certain demands. Those demands were of a humanitarian nature. Western nations wanted the Soviet Union and its Eastern European allies to agree to reunite families and to permit freer contact and exchange of ideas between people living on either side of the *Iron Curtain*. They also insisted that the Eastern bloc countries sign a human rights pact.

Eighteen months after Helsinki, Jimmy Carter was elected President of the United States. In his first address to the American people (January 1977) he indicated that he was going to take the human rights record of governments into account in conducting US foreign policy. 'Because we are free,' he declared, 'we can never be indifferent to the fate of freedom elsewhere.' Later, he was to describe human rights as 'the soul of American foreign policy'.

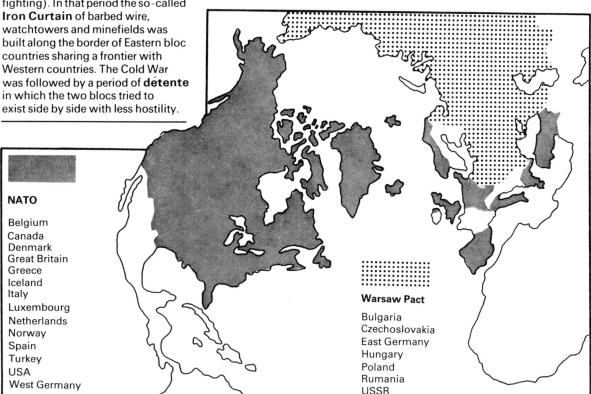

NATO

Belgium
Canada
Denmark
Great Britain
Greece
Iceland
Italy
Luxembourg
Netherlands
Norway
Spain
Turkey
USA
West Germany

Warsaw Pact

Bulgaria
Czechoslovakia
East Germany
Hungary
Poland
Rumania
USSR

Leonid Brezhnev, Soviet Communist Party General Secretary, and US President Gerald Ford after the European Conference on Security and Co-operation in Europe, at Helsinki, Finland, 1975. By the Helsinki agreement, Eastern bloc countries agreed to respect 'the effective exercise of civil, political...and other rights' and to conform to international agreements on human rights.

US President Jimmy Carter addressing the UN General Assembly in March 1977. He condemns 'torture' and 'deprivation of freedom' around the world and says that no nation 'can claim that mistreatment of its citizens is solely its own business'.

National interest

Governments often seem to allow questions of policy, security and national interest to override their position on human rights. They allow arms to be sold to countries where flagrant violations of rights take place. They make strategic alliances with countries with poor rights records. They refuse entry into the country of people they see as a security risk. Are such decisions in any way justifiable in the name of human rights?

Carter's pronouncements on human rights made headlines around the world in the late 1970s. There was an inevitable backlash. The Soviet Union and her allies, resenting his support for human rights groups in the Eastern bloc, accused the USA of interfering in their domestic politics. More important, however, was the fact that critics, both East and West, began to point out that the Carter administration was not, in every instance, practising what it preached. Whilst the Carter administration bewailed human rights violations in the Soviet Union and elsewhere, it gave financial aid to, permitted unrestricted trade with, and sold arms to states guilty of gross violations of human rights, such as Argentina, Indonesia and South Africa. Tackled by its critics, the US government defended its actions by arguing that national security and strategy sometimes had to override human rights considerations.

Judged by critics to be hollow and hypocritical, Carter's human rights policy nevertheless offers further evidence of the growing importance of human rights questions in the affairs of the 'global village'. Also, the fact that a superpower had pinned the 'human rights flag to its mast' inevitably pushed human rights further into the centre stage of international diplomacy. The area will remain a contentious one, not least because different countries interpret the idea of rights in different ways.

3 East and West, North and South

East, West, and the idea of freedom

The Soviet Union's readiness to sign human rights agreements such as the International Covenants of 1966 and the Helsinki Declaration of 1975 has puzzled some observers. Communists, they point out, have often rejected the notion of human rights as being a middle-class, Western idea giving an illusion of freedom to an exploited people while those in power go about accumulating wealth and property. Why then, they go on to ask, do Communist governments sign documents written in language more appropriate to Western democracies?

One approach is to explore what Western democracies and Communist states mean when they use the term 'human rights'. Such an exploration reveals a difference in priorities. Whereas Western countries place greater emphasis upon liberty-oriented rights, Communist governments talk principally in terms of security-oriented rights. Put another way, it could be said that the West gives pride of place to a person's *freedom to* do something while the Eastern bloc sets greater store upon guaranteeing a person's *freedom from* potentially harmful conditions. This is not necessarily to suggest that Western states dismiss social and economic rights or that Communist states reject civil and political rights. It is simply to say that each type of society decides upon its priorities, given its ideological standpoint. Communists would argue that civil and political rights are of secondary importance. How important, they would ask, is the right to vote once every five years if you are unemployed and living below the poverty line in a run-down inner-city part of Liverpool, New York or Sydney? What good is freedom of movement if you can't afford to

Run-down British housing in the 1980s.

travel anywhere? What value is the freedom to own property if you haven't any money? Liberty, they contend, is illusory without security. Communists also see Western governments' stress on protecting individual liberties as hypocritical. Human rights, Western-style, allow the privileged few to exploit and prosper at the expense of the majority. All too often individual rights are one person's right to benefit at the expense of another. For many, therefore, liberty is illusory without equality.

Western governments, for their part, accuse Communist bloc countries of cynicism in their attitude to human rights. Where is freedom, they ask, when critics of the government are put in labour camps or psychiatric hospitals for saying or writing what they think? Why does the Communist system offer people such limited opportunities to exercise their rights to independent thought and opinion? Why are there such strict limitations on people's freedom of travel and residence? The liberty-oriented rights of the individual must be protected if the state is to be prevented from being a dictatorship. Liberty is also vital for a healthy economy. Individuals need to be encouraged to do well and make profits for the economic good of everybody. The Communist system excludes reward for initiative and offers no incentive to the ambitious. Nor, they add, has the Eastern bloc proved it can 'deliver' economic and social securities to its people because their standard of living remains much below that enjoyed by a majority in the West.

East and West, therefore, have different priorities in mind in their pursuance of human rights. This leads to a somewhat different conception of the role of the state. In the West, the state sees its task as one of giving as much free rein as possible to the liberty of individuals, only stepping in when a person's freedom to act begins to harm the rights of others. The difficulty is one of deciding when that point has been reached. Western governments also see their role as one of achieving security-oriented rights for the individual through state provision of education, healthcare, pensions and welfare payments, the level of state involvement varying from country to country. Communist governments, on the other hand, hold that the social and economic rights of all citizens are best guaranteed through high levels of state intervention in most walks of life. Individuals, the argument goes, will benefit *equally* from an intrusive yet protective state system that cocoons citizens but under which liberty-oriented rights are necessarily curtailed.

Let us look at East and West Germany, the two states which emerged when the Soviet Union and the Western powers broke up Hitler's Germany in 1945. Workers in Communist East Germany do not face the prospect of a redundancy letter falling through their letter box. Unemployment is technically outlawed by the Constitution. Educational standards are high, prices of food and basic requirements have not risen for twenty years and they know that as long as they conform they will be protected from the cradle to the grave. There is, however, a price to pay. They are not allowed to criticise the government or the political system, move place of residence without permission, travel freely abroad or go on strike. Also, they will spend a lot of time queuing for other than basic food; clothes will be of indifferent quality and luxuries scarce. The more affluent West German workers are free to denounce their employer, the government and the political system; they are free to set up their own businesses and to travel where they please; they can join whatever political party they

'Turks out': a young *Gastarbeiter* removes racist graffiti in West Berlin.

want, although the state will ban them from certain jobs if they join an 'extreme' party (see Chapter 7). On the other hand, they may be unemployed tomorrow – as are approximately 2.4 million people out of a total population of 61 million (1986) in West Germany – and they may see the standard of living to which they have become accustomed slipping from their grasp. They live in a society where the loss of dignity caused by unemployment is leading to the growth of extremist political groups (including Fascist groups) and to the growth of hostile attitudes to foreign *Gastarbeiter*. Such 'guest workers' (mainly Turks) are none too sure that they have many rights in West German society.

Again, we see that there is no one single straightforward interpretation of the word 'freedom'. Both East and West assert they value 'freedom' and 'human rights' but mean something rather different when employing the term. Westerners condemn Soviet and other Eastern bloc governments for their attitude and actions towards dissidents (critics of the government) as a cruel denial of freedom. Those in the East reply by arguing that the state guarantees people their rights (securities) and so anybody criticising or trying to undermine the state is threatening the rights of fellow citizens. Given the Communist understanding of how rights are best achieved, the reply has its own logic whatever one's view of the often vicious way in which Eastern bloc governments deal with their critics (see Chapter 5).

Communist governments, therefore, say they are absolutely justified when they sign binding international agreements on human rights. Their record on rights (for which, read *securities*), they claim, is second to none.

Making the whole subject yet more complex is the fact that all international treaties on human rights acknowledge that people's possession of rights can never be absolute in practice. In 1973 Leonid Brezhnev, Soviet Communist Party General Secretary, defended the USSR's human rights record by pointing out that the International Covenant on Civil and Political Rights lays down that human rights are necessarily restricted by considerations such as 'national security, public order, public health or morals, or the rights and freedoms of others'. Restrictions on the civil and political rights of Soviet citizens, especially critics of the regime, were therefore in accord with international law, he claimed. The European Convention on Human Rights, likewise, makes it clear that rights may need to be restricted in the interests of national security and public safety and for the prevention of disorder or crime. There is growing evidence (see Chapter 7) that, as economic, social and political tensions grow, Western governments are increasingly trespassing on individual rights. When, for instance, does an issue begin to threaten 'public safety'? Who decides? Clearly, there is always the risk that those in authority will re-define the border line in what is a very grey area.

North, South, and human rights

Western doubts over the Eastern bloc's commitment to human rights often extends to the governments of many 'Third World' countries. Although African, Asian, Caribbean and South American states in large numbers have signed the Universal Declaration, many in the West hold that they pay little more than lip service to the notion of human rights. They point out that Third World countries – including many

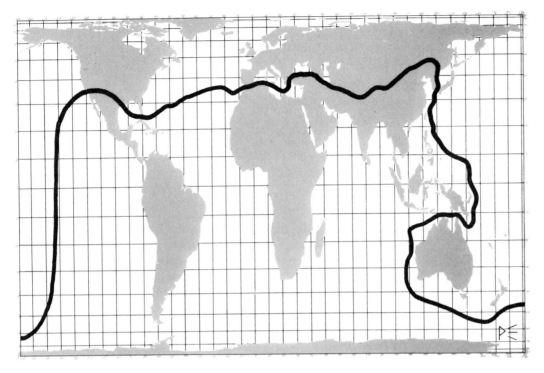

The division between the developed nations and the Third World is sometimes called the North–South divide, for the reason suggested by this map based on the Peters projection. The map aims to show the true proportion of land surface area of different countries.

'Developed' countries are wealthy, industrialised nations, principally those of North America, Europe, Australia and Japan. Poor and underdeveloped nations of Central and South America, Africa and Asia are known as the 'Third World'. They hold three-quarters of the world's population but earn only one-fifth of its income.

In the 'poor South' life expectancy is less than 48; each year over 15 million children under five die and another 10 million suffer brain damage, deformity or stunted growth on account of malnutrition or starvation. (1980 figures)

that have ratified the Universal Declaration – have witnessed more than their fair share of gross human rights violations (see Chapters 4 and 6), that women and minorities often fare very badly, and that many are one-party states or governed by dictators. The response of some Third World governments has been to point to the extreme poverty facing their peoples. Given the situation, they see their major priority as the achievement of basic human rights, especially the provision of basic needs for survival. The achievement of basic rights, they argue, is a necessary pre-condition to the enjoyment of a wider spread of liberty- and security-oriented rights. In the pursuance of basic rights, individual liberties must sometimes be sacrificed to the 'greater good'. Also, while their countries remain poor they will not be in a position to provide securities of the type provided by the welfare systems of the industrialised nations.

Some authoritarian regimes in the Third World justify their style of government by referring to the grave economic circumstances with which they are confronted. Single-party government reduces argument and is thus, they claim, an aid to efficiency. As such, it actually improves the chances of implementing the basic rights of the people. Democracy, they assert, is an envied luxury enjoyed by wealthy societies. Spokesmen of many 'Third World' countries also remind their critics that they have been independent for less than thirty years. The combined task of welding a people into a nation and meeting their urgent needs requires authoritarian government.

There are also *cultural* reasons why many Third World countries tend to pay less heed to individual liberties. Asian philosophies and religions in particular, such as Buddhism and Taoism, have traditionally emphasised the concepts of harmony and order within society. Characteristically, they have also laid great emphasis upon an individual's *duty* to avoid disturbing harmonious social relationships through self-assertion. Western observers who choose to measure the rights record of Third World societies using individual liberty as their yardstick may, thus, be guilty of judging another culture by the standards of their own.

It is also important to point out that the human rights record of certain Western states has not been all that exemplary. North American Indians, Australian Aborigines, the Sami of Norway, ethnic minorities in Britain and migrant workers in West Germany have all suffered at the hands of government (see Chapter 7). Nor is it fair to ignore the record of achievement in the Third World in terms of liberty-oriented rights. It is worth noting, for example, that India is the world's largest democracy and that many African societies have a vibrant tradition of *palaver*, conferences at which political and legal disputes are settled by free and open discussion.

Worlds apart: whilst most people favour human rights in theory, putting the theory into practice produces a knot of contending views.

1 US government spokesman
Individuals should be free from tyranny and oppression. Arbitrary arrest, detention and torture we find abhorrent. We will continue to protest loudly when human rights violations are brought to our attention. Sometimes we may find it necessary to show we mean business, by cutting back aid to offenders. But that is not always possible; especially in places like Indonesia and South Korea, which are important for our national security. In general it's just not good business to make our commercial dealings dependent on our view of human rights.

3 African socialist leader
The most basic human right is the right to life itself. In my country people die through lack of clean water, food and basic medical care. These are our priorities. If we have to silence those who would seek to undermine our unity and national goals, then so be it.

2 Soviet official
I would suggest that the USA look at their own country first. They can't even guarantee the most basic of rights to many of their citizens – the right to employment and the right to benefit from the economy of the nation. Our Soviet system of socialism is a true democracy which gives everyone the opportunity to participate in the economy. The state provides for our needs, and we work together to support the state.

4 Latin-American General
That is precisely our position. But in this country we believe the surest way to economic development is the free-market system. Unfortunately there are subversive Marxist forces that want to destroy our great nation. We can and will provide our citizens with employment and a decent income. But we cannot succeed in granting basic human rights until revolutionaries are rounded up and their anti-Christian beliefs expunged from our country.

6 Australian Aborigine
We have lived here for thousands of years, roaming freely, and living off the land. Since the European settlement our freedom has been curtailed. The whites want to destroy what little land we have left by digging for minerals. Don't we have rights too?

5 Latin-American peasant
Well, I'm as much a Christian as you. But as far as I can see, your so-called free market hasn't done much for the poor. The military generals and rich landowners are doing well. But we can barely afford our next meal. Maybe if we could have our own land to grow food, things would improve. Instead, a US corporation grows fruit which is exported to the rich world. And then, when we peasants get together to demand our rights, you call us communists and arrest us. So your system takes away our rights twice over.

4   Human rights in Latin America

Rich and poor in Latin America

So near and yet so far: shanties in the foreground, with modern offices and apartment blocks in the distance, Sao Paulo, Brazil.

A visit to the commercial centre of the Chilean capital, Santiago, would reveal a bustling, modern shopping area that would stand comparison with any wealthy Northern city. One would see hundreds of smart shops bristling with every modern appliance from electric toothbrushes to German, Japanese and American hi-fi systems, clothes from the best Parisian designers, stylish shoes from Italy and chocolates and whisky from Britain. Such imported luxuries are, however, beyond the buying power of all but a handful of citizens of Santiago: the rich minority who live in exclusive suburbs in luxury houses with spectacular views of the snow-capped mountains surrounding the city. While there are large numbers of less wealthy but 'comfortable' citizens, most Chileans find it a struggle to afford basic food items. In Santiago, the majority can be found living in the *poblaciones*, the inner-city housing estates and poor quarters, or in the rapidly growing shanty towns on the outskirts of the city. In the latter, the better-off wage-earners have built wooden huts while the unemployed and new arrivals from the countryside build shacks out of cardboard boxes, old crates, plastic sheeting and newspaper. The roads are muddy or dusty depending on the season; most people share the few communal taps; sanitary facilities are primitive and recreational and healthcare facilities virtually non-existent.

Such striking contrasts of wealth and poverty can be found throughout the length and breadth of Latin America. The inequalities were well highlighted at the time of the spectacular World Cup Finals held in Argentina in 1978. Seven hundred million US dollars were spent on staging the Finals; a new stadium was built in Buenos Aires, the capital city, and facilities for colour television were installed in the country. Away from the eyes of the television cameras, the rat-infested shanty towns on the route to Buenos Aires' airport were razed to the ground by bulldozers so as to give visitors as good an impression as possible of the host country. The occupants of the shanty towns were offered no compensation for disturbance or help in finding alternative accommodation.

The striking contrast between the type of life enjoyed by a tiny wealthy minority in Latin America and the squalor, misery and lack of opportunity which is the lot of the majority raises important questions. From every source there is irresistible evidence that social and economic conditions fall short of those laid down in Article 25 of the Universal Declaration that 'everyone has the right to a standard of living adequate for the health and well-being of himself and his family, including food, clothing, housing and medical care and necessary social services'. Latin America is rich in natural resources. The problem is that the benefits arising from those resources are distributed in a very unequal way.

Paradoxically, the very attraction of those food and mineral resources may have played a part in worsening the lot of most Latin-American people. Although the Latin-American countries won their independence from Spain and Portugal in the nineteenth century, after three centuries of colonial rule, they still found themselves, to varying degrees, economically tied to Europe, and increasingly to the United States. This economic 'dependence' on the 'First World', and the domination of foreign investment and foreign ownership, is often blamed as the cause for the fragility of the economies and the widespread poverty in Latin America. By concentrating on producing just one raw material – Colombian coffee, Guatemalan bananas, or Chilean copper, for example – and by responding to the demand from Europe and the USA, Latin-American countries thereby fail to develop an agricultural and industrial economy which is geared towards their own local needs, and which could better weather the storm in times of world depression. Since the turn of the century US companies have often bought vast areas of land in Latin America to grow food for the markets of North America. Three US fruit *transnationals* (United Brands, Del Monte and the Standard Fruit and Steamship Company), for example, now control seventy per cent of the Central-American banana trade. Foreign business people and the local collaborative élites grow rich on the profits.

It is worth considering, however, whether there really was any viable alternative for Latin-American economic development. Some would argue that it is not just the economic pressures of the 'First World' that are to blame: with small domestic markets, a limited supply of fuel, and a shortage of skilled and unskilled labour, there never was a realistic chance that Latin-American economies could have diversified in the same way as in the USA and Europe. And indeed some of the more developed Latin-American countries such as Argentina were not coerced, but chose to specialise as primary producers (prior to the 1929 world depression), because it was profitable.

On arrival in the nearest town or city, Latin-American peasants now join the ranks of the unemployed simply because there are too many people arriving for the few jobs available. The chance of employment will, more likely than not, depend upon securing work in one of the mines or factories opened or taken over by US or European transnational companies since the 1960s, such as Ford's car plant in Buenos Aires, Argentina, or the Volkswagen factory in Sao Bernardo, Brazil. The

A cartoonist's view of US involvement in Latin America. What do you think of this viewpoint?

Transnational companies are companies with operations spreading across (hence *trans)* many countries. They are often called **multinational** companies. It is estimated that they now control between a quarter and a third of total world production.

Country	Life expectancy at birth (in years)		Infant aged 0–1 mortality rate per thousand		Population per physician	
	1960	1981	1960	1981	1960	1981
Australia	71	74	20	10	750	560
United Kingdom	71	74	23	12	940	650
USA	70	75	26	12	750	520
USSR	68	72	33	n/a	560	280
Argentina	65	71	61	44	740	530
Brazil	55	64	118	75	2,670	1,700
Chile	57	68	114	42	1,780	1,920
Cuba	63	73	66	19	1,060	700
El Salvador	51	63	136	75	5,260	3,040
Guatemala	47	59	92	66	4,420	8,600
Honduras	46	59	145	86	12,620	3,120
Peru	47	58	163	85	1,910	1,390

World Bank, *World Development Report*, 1983
The above figures are from official sources and need to be treated with caution. This is particularly the case with health statistics (e.g. the definition of 'physician' can differ between countries)

Inflation (%)

Country	1976	1977	1978	1979
Argentina	443.2	176.1	175.5	170.0
Brazil	41.9	43.7	38.7	77.2
Chile	211.9	92.0	40.1	38.9
Colombia	17.4	30.0	17.4	*25.0
Mexico	16.1	26.4	17.5	*20.0
Paraguay	4.5	9.3	10.8	*20.0
Peru	33.5	38.1	57.8	67.0
Uruguay	50.7	58.1	44.6	80.0
Venezuela	7.6	7.7	7.2	*20.0

Inter-American Development Bank   *estimate

transnationals, attracted to Latin America by the large pool of labour available, pay very low wages, wages that have dwindled in real value as inflation has continued to rocket. The average wage earned in the Latin-American subcontinent is insufficient to feed a family to a sound nutritional standard. As a result malnutrition is widespread in what is a major food-producing area of the world and infant mortality rates are tragically high.

The stark and bitter contrast between the rich and poor of Latin America – the failure to ensure the basic security-oriented rights of a large majority of citizens – accounts for the high level of political unrest and instability in the subcontinent. Unrest has expressed itself in demonstrations, trade-union agitation, the re-occupation of land owned by the big landowners and, sometimes, in the election of centre or left-wing politicians promising a programme of social and economic reform.

All too often, however, the wishes of the people, as expressed in the ballot box, have been overturned by the military representing the interests of the wealthy who feel their position threatened by the prospect of reform. Chile is a case in point. In 1970, Salvador Allende was elected head of a 'Popular Unity' government. The broad aim of

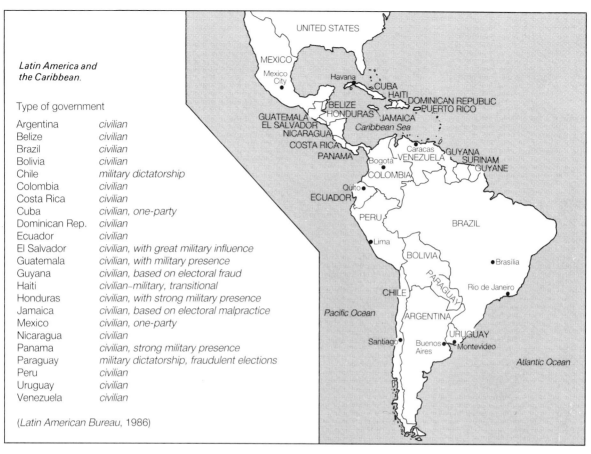

Latin America and
the Caribbean.

Type of government

Argentina	*civilian*
Belize	*civilian*
Brazil	*civilian*
Bolivia	*civilian*
Chile	*military dictatorship*
Colombia	*civilian*
Costa Rica	*civilian*
Cuba	*civilian, one-party*
Dominican Rep.	*civilian*
Ecuador	*civilian*
El Salvador	*civilian, with great military influence*
Guatemala	*civilian, with military presence*
Guyana	*civilian, based on electoral fraud*
Haiti	*civilian–military, transitional*
Honduras	*civilian, with strong military presence*
Jamaica	*civilian, based on electoral malpractice*
Mexico	*civilian, one-party*
Nicaragua	*civilian*
Panama	*civilian, strong military presence*
Paraguay	*military dictatorship, fraudulent elections*
Peru	*civilian*
Uruguay	*civilian*
Venezuela	*civilian*

(*Latin American Bureau*, 1986)

'Popular Unity' was to distribute the wealth of Chile more fairly by means of a programme of land reform and nationalisation of industry and mining, and by promoting education, housing and welfare facilities. In 1973 a military coup, backed by the wealthier sections of Chilean society and US transnationals, overthrew Allende's government, killing him and thousands of his supporters. The military took over.

'Disappearances' and torture

On 20 July 1974, a member of the Chilean international cycling team, Sergio Tormen, was arrested by officers of the DINA (secret police) in his bicycle workshop in Santiago. His fourteen-year-old brother was arrested the same day but released after questioning by the DINA. On 27 November 1974, the newspaper *El Mercurio*, reported that, according to the military authorities, 'Tormen seems to have gone to Argentina secretly,' and added that he was only detained by the authorities between 20 July and 5 August. Since his arrest, Tormen has not been seen by his family or friends.

On 24 August 1976, the children and daughter-in-law of a well-known opponent of the Argentinian regime, Juan Gelman, were abducted from their homes by men claiming to be Federal Police. Juan Gelman was abroad at the time and had publicly denounced the military regime. Gelman's daughter, Nora, in poor health after a road accident, was released ten days later but his son, Marcelo, and Marcelo's pregnant wife, Claudia, were not.

Disappeared sportsman: Sergio Tormen.

'**Disappearances**' are not just a Latin-American phenomenon although some of the worst examples have happened there. Amnesty International has recorded disappearances world-wide. In Africa there were disappearances in Uganda under Amin (President 1971–9) and Obote (President 1966–71, 1980–5); and sporadic cases have been reported in Ethiopia during the 1980s. Disappearances have also been rife in Asia – for example in the Philippines under Marcos (President 1965–86); and in Afghanistan (1978–9). Disappearances have been recorded under current regimes in the Middle East too – for example in Morocco under Hassan II (King 1961–); and Syria under Hasez al Assad (re-elected President for his third seven-year term in 1985).

Torture

An act by which severe suffering or pain, whether physical or mental, is inflicted on a person to obtain a confession, information or as a form of punishment.

Sergio Tormen, Marcelo and Claudia Gelman are but three names from a long list of 'disappeared' people in Latin America. Nobody knows quite how long the list is. After the coup in Chile in 1973, disappearances became a regular event just as they did after the military coup in Argentina in 1976. Amnesty International, the watchdog body for 'prisoners of conscience' (see Chapter 10), has evidence concerning 1,500 people arrested in Chile after the coup who have since disappeared and also estimates that some 15,000 Argentinian citizens were made to disappear between 1976 and 1983. In Guatemala, where disappearances have been a regular feature since the 1960s, an estimated 15,000 people vanished without trace between 1970 and 1975 and approximately 5,000 between 1978 and 1981. In El Salvador, nearly 5,000 people disappeared in 1982 alone. Disappearances have also been recorded in Bolivia, Mexico, Paraguay and Uruguay. The immediate intention on the part of the government involved is to silence and rid itself of critics and opponents either by causing them, or those near and dear to them, to disappear. The broader intention is to intimidate the entire population by creating an atmosphere of fear. A policy of disappearance is seen as convenient because it evades legal formalities such as having to take people to court and justifying their arrest. It is also convenient because the government involved simply denies that it has a particular person in its custody. Such a denial makes it extremely difficult for human rights campaigners, lawyers or the international community to aid the person concerned. The disappeared person, in a sense, becomes a 'non-person' deprived of all legal protection.

For those arrested, whether or not they ultimately join the ranks of the disappeared, the likelihood is that they will be tortured. *Torture* is widely practised in Latin America. It is carried out by both the police and the military, the government either actively encouraging or making little or no effort to prevent it.

The aim of using torture is to gain information useful to authorities in their efforts to stamp out 'subversion'. It is also employed as a further means of intimidating the population in general. A number of those tortured are eventually released and their story then circulates. Less frequently, it has been used to extract a confession prior to a public trial.

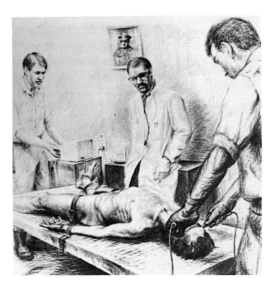

DINA agents in Chile torturing a victim: an artist's impression, based on the testimony of former victims, shows electrical torture. A doctor stands by to monitor the effects.

Amnesty International, the UN Commission of Human Rights and other organisations have been able to accumulate a horrific body of evidence concerning the use of torture in Latin America.

The 1983 Amnesty International report, *Torture in Chile*, describes the experiences of a nineteen-year-old social worker during the nineteen days she spent in the custody of the CNI (the secret police founded in 1977 when the DINA was disbanded). She was arrested in Santiago without a warrant and taken to the CNI detention centre in the city. During her interrogation she was slapped all over her body, punched in the face, breasts and abdomen and kicked on the buttocks and thighs. She was later electrically tortured by being stretched on a metal bed (known as *la parrilla*, the grill) with hands and feet bound; shocks were applied to her temples, chest, heels and vagina. On the eighth day, she was kicked and raped by four men. Some time afterwards, she was told that the man she had been living with had been killed. She was then taken to a room and forced to lie facing a decomposing naked male corpse with a towel covering its head. She was told that the corpse was that of her boyfriend (this she knew to be a lie given the body's height and build). At one point the towel was removed from the decomposing face. Later she was put in a room of rats but escaped them by jumping on a bed. Throughout her ordeal she was blindfolded except when being sexually tortured and when confronting the corpse. For the first fourteen days at the CNI detention centre, she was also partially deprived of sleep.

The account given above is from someone who lived to tell the tale. Many of those arrested by the police or the military or by paramilitary groups lose their lives. Mass graves have been unearthed in Argentina, Chile, El Salvador and Guatemala. Tortured and mutilated bodies have also been found in ravines, at roadsides, on rubbish dumps and washed up on coasts.

Soldiers burning bodies by the roadside near Zacatecoluca in El Salvador (about 70 kms from the capital), 1981. Opposition leaders said that the bodies were of civilian people killed by the government; soldiers said they were guerillas.

The response of military regimes to accusations of gross violations of basic human rights has been to deny that rights have been violated to anything like the extent that their critics maintain; they have also argued that they are involved in a war against 'subversion' and that, in time of war, rights violations are unavoidable. The Argentinian military regime (1976–83) talked of a 'dirty war' against 'subversion' (the latter encompassing, it seems, those involved in both peaceful and armed struggle against the government). The disappeared, it argued, were the inevitable casualties of the 'dirty war'.

The story of disappearance, torture and killing described above involves a direct violation of basic human rights which can be condemned irrespective of one's political stand. Basic rights directly violated include the right to life, the right to recognition as a person before the law, freedom from arbitrary arrest, detention and exile, the right to a fair trial, freedom from torture and the right to some liberty and security. Other rights are also indirectly infringed, such as freedom of opinion and expression, and the right to join a trade union. Although there are laws throughout much of Latin America limiting the freedom of the press and the activities of trade unions, it is an open question as to whether such laws are really needed by the regimes concerned. The 'climate of fear' created by disappearances and torture is such that people are afraid to exercise rights to which they are entitled.

Torture, disappearances and the economic exploitation of the people in Latin America are the outcome of a number of factors. They include the imposition of military rule (answerable to no independent legal or democratic process), the alliance between the military and the wealthy and the virtually unrestricted freedom of the wealthy to exercise their right of ownership. We are left with a number of related questions. Firstly, what reforms in the system of government would enable societies in the region to be more fairly and humanely organised? Secondly, would government be justified in limiting the rights of the propertied? If so, when would the point be reached at which government efforts to create a more equitable society would eat too heavily into the individual rights of the wealthy?

The USA and human rights in Latin America

With the exception of Nicaragua, the regimes of Latin America are actively supported by the United States. The question arises as to how the USA squares that support with its frequently declared championship of human rights.

Some of the answer lies in the Western view that Communism is an aggressive force bent upon extending its sway and influence wherever it can. The military regimes of Latin America are strongly anti-Communist. They therefore receive US backing, as do oppressive regimes in Asia (see Chapter 6), as buffers against the spread of Communism. In both areas the 'domino' theory continues to influence US policy; the idea that if one country falls to Communism then others will follow in turn, thus extending the influence of the Soviet Union in the world. The Communist revolution in Cuba in 1959 continues to haunt US policy and her fears about the spread of the 'infection' grew sharper when the Nicaraguan dictator, Somosa, was overthrown by the Cuban-supported Socialist Sandinista Front in 1979.

US troops invading Grenada, 1983, backed by troops from a number of Caribbean countries. President Reagan justified the invasion by arguing that Grenada's leadership was turning the country into an undemocratic, Communist state, and by pointing to the build-up of Cuban military personnel and arms on the island. Grenada, he said, was rapidly becoming a threat to the USA, and a base for Communist subversion in the region. The Covenant on Civil and Political Rights gives all nations the right to self-determination (the right to work out their own problems and future). Was the invasion of Grenada justified or not?

The US invasion of the small Caribbean island of Grenada in 1983 to overthrow a four-year old Socialist regime offers a further example of the US preoccupation with the threat of Communist expansion.

The spectre of Communism and Soviet domination thus offers some explanation of why the USA is prepared to support regimes made up of military leaders who have been described as 'indistinguishable from the war criminals hanged at Nuremberg after World War II'. For further explanation, we need to look at the level of US economic involvement and investment in Latin America as referred to earlier in this chapter. Economically, the region is a vital one for the markets and raw materials it offers to the USA and as an area offering cheap labour for US transnationals. US business interests do not, of course, support torture and disappearances. But those interests are attracted by regimes that offer unrestricted possibilities for making a profit. Interestingly, economists have found that US aid to Latin America tends to flow more readily to those states with high levels of human rights violations.

'National security' considerations and the high level of US economic involvement in Latin America, therefore, help to explain why the USA gives a fairly low priority to rights considerations in its own backyard, in spite of its declared international commitment to human rights. A right-wing oppressive regime, paying scant regard to citizens' rights is, it seems, preferable to a regime, however popular, which might threaten US strategic or economic interests. This is not to imply moral superiority in the Soviet Union's international role. The USSR has trampled upon the right to self-determination of Eastern bloc countries, notably in Hungary in 1956, and in Czechoslovakia in 1968; its invasion of Afghanistan in 1979 on the flimsiest of pretexts offers further evidence that when the strategic and economic chips are down, human rights count for all too little in major-power policy-making.

5 Human rights in the Soviet Union

Soviet law and the dissidents

In 1976 a Russian worker, Mikhail Kukobaka, was put in a psychiatric hospital for distributing copies of the Universal Declaration of Human Rights around his home-town of Mogilev in the Ukraine. The psychiatrist who diagnosed Kukobaka's 'complaint' said that he suffered from 'a mania for the reconstruction of society'. Another symptom of his 'mental illness' was that he had hung a religious picture and photographs of two leading Russian dissidents over his bed in the hostel where he was living. Those responsible for Kukobaka's case described the Universal Declaration as 'anti-Soviet literature'.

The Soviet Union abstained in the United Nations vote on the Universal Declaration in 1948. Since that time, however, the Soviet government has signed some important international documents on human rights, including the Helsinki Conference Final Act of 1975 under which participants agreed to respect human rights and fundamental freedoms. The new Soviet Constitution of 1977 seemed, on the face of it, to reflect the Helsinki Declaration, Article 34, stating that 'equality of rights of citizens of the USSR shall be ensured in all fields of economic, political, social and cultural life'.

But the actual laws by which the Soviet Union is governed can be used to stifle those who disagree with the government. For example, citizens may not exercise their rights 'to the detriment of the interests of society or the state'. It is official bodies who decide what those 'interests' are. Freedom of expression and freedom of association are guaranteed as long as the freedoms are used in 'the interests of the people and in order to strengthen and develop the socialist system'. Soviet law also states that citizens have 'the right to conduct religious worship or atheistic propaganda' (but *not* religious propaganda).

THE SILENT MAJORITY

© AUTH, THE PHILADELPHIA INQUIRER, THE WASHINGTON POST WRITERS' GROUP

It is when one comes to examine the treatment meted out to dissidents that the conditions described above acquire real significance.

The Soviet Criminal Code forbids 'anti-Soviet agitation and propaganda' and the 'dissemination of fabrications [lies] known to be false which defame the Soviet state and social system'. A first offence for 'anti-Soviet agitation and propaganda' carries a sentence of up to twelve years' imprisonment and exile. 'Dissemination of fabrications' is less severely punished. The law is used to silence critics of the government or its policies. For example, members of minority nationalities who criticise the lack of freedom given to minorities are liable to arrest and imprisonment for having 'slandered' the Soviet state and its policies. Likewise, members of minorities such as Jews who apply for emigration are liable to imprisonment because the reasons they give for wanting to leave the country are held to be 'slanderous'.

Letters of complaint to the authorities can also lead to a prison sentence. In August 1978 Nikolai Shatalov was sentenced to eighteen months' imprisonment for 'dissemination of fabrications'. Since 1976 Shatalov and his family had been trying to emigrate. In the autumn of that year his wife was put in a psychiatric hospital for four months after visiting the American Embassy in Moscow for advice on emigration. In March 1977 Shatalov's son was sent to prison for two years for refusing to do compulsory military service. Shatalov then wrote to Leonid Brezhnev, Soviet Party Leader (1964–82), complaining about human rights violations and criticising the Soviet system. He was jailed as a result of his complaint.

The Criminal Code also forbids 'participation in an anti-Soviet organisation'. This law is, from time to time, used to break up dissident or human rights groups and to imprison their members.

Religious groups in the Soviet Union are governed by the 'legislation on cults' (three decrees on religion dating from 1919, 1929 and 1966). The legislation lays down that all religious congregations must be registered with the state-run Council for Religious Affairs. The Council has the power to refuse – and withdraw – registration without giving a reason. A congregation also needs the permission of the local Soviet authority before it can use a building for purposes of prayer and worship. Religious practices are forbidden in state or public places.

The Criminal Code lays down stiff penalties for breaking the 'legislation on cults', one of the most serious crimes being to meet as an unregistered, and therefore illegal, congregation. Religious believers are also persecuted in ways which have no basis in law. They are often discriminated against at their place of work; they are sometimes refused adequate housing; they are frequently abused in the newspapers with no right of reply. In education, religious children are often denied equal opportunities and teachers hold them up to scorn and ridicule before their classmates. Believers, Christian, Jewish, Moslem and Buddhist, have become 'a huge group of second-class citizens' in the Soviet Union.

There have also been numerous cases of the children of religious believers being taken away from their parents. In Soviet law, one duty of parents is to educate children 'in the spirit of the moral code of the builder of communism'. If they fail to carry out their parental duties, the state can deprive parents of their children. Inevitably, religious parents do not train their children to deny the existence of God, as the state philosophy requires, and so they face the constant threat of their family being broken up. A horrifying and well-documented case occurred in 1966 when the two elder children of Baptists, Ivan and

Joseph Begun, Jewish scientist and mathematician, was sacked from his important state post when he applied to emigrate to Israel in 1971. Unable to obtain a new post fitting his talents, he took low-paid jobs working for Jewish organisations until his arrest for 'parasitism' in 1977. He was sentenced to two years internal exile.

Nadezhda Sloboda, were removed from their parents and sent to a boarding school. Badly treated, the children ran away and returned home only to be carried off again, screaming, by the police. Soon afterwards, Nadezhda was sentenced to four years in prison and in 1970 the other three children were removed from home.

Another feature of Russian treatment of dissident and religious groups is the use of imprecise criminal laws to suppress activities and opinions which do not have state approval. The law on 'hooliganism' is an example of this. 'Hooliganism' is defined as 'intentional actions violating public order in a coarse manner and expressing a clear disrespect towards society'. Such a loose definition enables the authorities to prosecute dissidents for a wide range of activities. Similarly the law against 'parasitism' (i.e. living off others without making a contribution) has been used to imprison those critical of the government.

Freedom of movement is heavily restricted in the USSR. Soviet citizens may only leave the country with the permission of the authorities. As mentioned earlier, those applying to emigrate risk trial and imprisonment for 'anti-Soviet slander'. They also run the risk of being prosecuted for breaking the passport regulations. Would-be emigrants have, in some cases, followed regulations by submitting their passports along with their emigration papers only to be arrested and imprisoned for being without their passport (which is a citizen's basic identity document in the USSR). Movement *within* the Soviet Union is also restricted. Passport regulations insist that all citizens have to be registered with the local authority for the area where they live. They cannot change place of residence without obtaining the permission of the authorities in both their present and intended places of residence. Permission can be refused on a variety of grounds.

The punishment of dissidents

The arrest of Soviet dissidents usually only occurs after a period of police harassment and surveillance, the intention of which is to silence them so that an arrest is unnecessary. House searches, dismissal from employment, hostile articles in local or national newspapers and brief spells of imprisonment on petty charges are commonly used. If such techniques do not silence the dissident, arrest follows. Lawyers are not permitted to see the prisoners until the official investigation is complete, and friends and relatives usually find it impossible to get into the courtroom for the trial.

On being convicted, most dissidents end up in camps where there is emphasis on 're-education' of the prisoner.

Dissidents often consider the journey to and from the labour camp as the most horrific aspect of a prison sentence. Many camps are in remote parts of the Soviet Union, such as Siberia, and the rail journey can take a month or more. The wagons used to carry prisoners may be overcrowded with poor ventilation, and there is not enough food. An example of prisoner ill-treatment during transportation occurred during a heatwave in 1972. One prisoner of conscience recalls:

Fifteen people in a sleeping compartment. Everybody bathed in sweat. Food spoiled. For two days they did not take prisoners to the lavatory. People had to use the corridors. The windows were sealed shut. Only at the end of the deportation did they open the windows a little, but it did not help. People were lying naked on the floor. Dirt. Stink. Suffocation. One man died during deportation. It was a terrible torture.

The labour camps themselves have barrack-type accommodation which is often overcrowded. Prisoners complain of lack of privacy, lack of ventilation, little or no heating, constant noise from the loudspeaker system and inadequate toilet facilities. The food is insufficient for the hard labour expected of them. Only one blanket is permitted per inmate even though the camps are situated in locations which are extremely cold – well below freezing – in winter. Most dissidents are also sentenced to a period of 'internal exile' to follow after their labour camp sentence. Internal exile involves 'socially useful labour' in some isolated town or region of the USSR, such as Gorki, and usually with a very severe climate.

A labour camp which forms part of the Mordovian complex of corrective labour colonies (photograph smuggled out of the Soviet Union).

A rare, secretly shot photograph of an identified prisoner, Eugeny Nikolayev, at the window of Kashchenko Mental Hospital, 1977. In Soviet psychiatric hospitals, powerful tranquilising drugs are used by the 'cops in white coats' to punish dissidents and encourage them 'to reform their ways'.

The Helsinki Watch Groups

To dissidents, the Helsinki Declaration of 1975 provided an opportunity to campaign for human rights in the Soviet Union. Suddenly, minority nationalist groups, religious and political dissidents could unite around a common document signed by their own government. In May 1976 an unofficial Helsinki Watch Group was set up in Moscow to monitor Soviet observance of the human rights clauses of the Declaration. By April 1977 similar groups had sprung up in the Ukraine, Lithuania, Georgia and Armenia. The Watch Groups operated openly and *Samizdat* (unofficially published) literature on human rights issues became more frequent.

The Soviet authorities, embarrassed by the world-wide attention given to the Watch Groups, clamped down on their activities. In 1977 Yuri Orlov, founder of the Moscow Group, was sentenced to seven years in a labour camp to be followed by five years of internal exile. (Orlov was released in 1986 in a deal made between the USSR and USA.) By 1982 almost all the original members of the Group were serving long prison or labour camp sentences whilst Andrei Sakharov, the nuclear scientist, was banished with his wife to Gorki, a city closed to foreign visitors, and was only allowed to return from exile in 1987.

Psychiatric hospitals

One technique used to stifle the Helsinki Watch Groups and other dissident groups has been forcible confinement in Soviet psychiatric hospitals. About 200 people are estimated to have been confined between 1975 and 1979 not because they were mentally ill but because they chose to exercise their human rights. Amongst the reasons given by the authorities to justify forcible psychiatric treatment have been 'writing complaints to government authorities', 'criticising the government in the presence of workmates' and 'persistently making religious craft articles'. The diagnoses offered by officially appointed psychiatrists have included 'nervous exhaustion brought on by her search for justice' 'reformist ideas' and 'schizophrenia with religious delirium'. There are two types of psychiatric hospital to which a dissident can be sent. 'Special' psychiatric hospitals are maximum-security institutions and are run like prisons. Confinement there is long-term and the treatment of 'patients' has been shown to be, in many cases, vicious. 'Ordinary' psychiatric hospitals house short-term inmates and the treatment is less extreme.

Does Moscow deliver on security-oriented rights?

Communist thinking on human rights was discussed in Chapter 3. There it was suggested that human rights are interpreted by Communist governments as primarily being social and economic *securities*, to be shared equally by all citizens and guaranteed by the state. It is this particular prioritisation of rights that is often used in justification of the Soviet stance on liberty-oriented rights and dissidence. Any criticism of the state, its policies and workings is held to be an attack on the rights of others since the state provides everybody's rights (securities).

To what extent does the Soviet Union achieve social and economic well-being for its citizens? The question is a difficult one to answer for two reasons. In the first place, information on the USSR is hard to come by and has to be pieced together from a variety of sources. In the second place, we have to be clear that when we compare Soviet and Western achievement in the field of social and economic rights we are not comparing runners that started equal in the same race. The Soviet Union dates from only 1917 and inherited poor housing and inadequate and grossly unequal systems of education, healthcare and welfare, with enormous variations in standard of living between one state and another. This burden of poverty and inequality had to be tackled within a country of immense size that had undergone comparatively little industrial development. Bearing in mind these two points – and also the terrible destruction and huge loss of life during the First and Second World Wars – let us examine some aspects of the social and economic rights record of the Soviet Union.

In 1920 a Soviet minimum housing standard of nine square metres of space per person was established. More than half a century later, the national average was 7·6 square metres – about a half of the space available per person in Western European cities. In other words, in the 1970s the great majority of Soviet people were still not housed in conformity with health standards set fifty years previously. Against this dismal picture has to be set the fact that since the 1950s the Soviet Union has built more new units of housing than any other country in the world (roughly 44 million units between 1956 and 1975). Despite the scale of effort new accommodation in Soviet cities is modest by Western standards while housing standards in rural areas remain very low. Thirty kilometres from the centre of Moscow, villages can be found without modern sanitation facilities.

A similar picture of great achievements and great shortcomings is evident in the field of healthcare. The Soviet Union has made huge strides forward in health provision since the 1917 Revolution and this has led to steep declines in infant and general mortality rates (see the table on page 28). Looking behind the statistics, however, we find that

Modern residential district at Obolon, Kiev, 1980s. The vast scale of the Soviet housing programme has barely kept up with population growth and the migration of people from countryside to town; so far, it has been unable to replace the housing stock devastated in the Second World War.

improvements made have not been as staggering as the figures indicate. The Soviet health system, evidence suggests, is beset by overworked and low-paid doctors, shortages of medicine, poor equipment and hospital organisation. Overcrowding and delays in being admitted into hospital are a frequent complaint amongst Soviets requiring non-emergency operations. These shortcomings aside, the majority of Soviets seem to regard their state healthcare system as a very positive feature of Communism. As the cost to the private patient rocketed in the USA and in other Western countries lacking national health schemes during the economic crisis of the late 1970s and early 1980s, Soviet officials were not slow to point out the freedom from crippling medical bills enjoyed by the Soviet citizen.

A negative aspect of Soviet life from the point of view of the ordinary citizen is the scarcity of food and consumer goods. Items are permanently out of stock or their appearance in the shops is unpredictable. Goods are distributed down a 'league table' of cities starting with Moscow so that smaller cities and towns often fare very badly. The meat departments in small city food stores, for instance, may run out of supplies of fresh meat for most of the winter period. The haphazard appearance of food and consumer goods in shops – the result of an economy geared to the development of heavy industry and to military build-up – has led to that constant feature of Soviet life: the queue. Discontent with the situation is tempered by an appreciation that there have been great improvements in the post-war period. Between 1950 and 1970 Soviet food consumption per head doubled, actual income in the wage packet quadrupled and the working week was shortened.

In the areas of housing, health and food, there is clear evidence that the Soviet Union has been able to deliver significant improvements in social and economic rights. The degree of progress attained is, however, debatable and depends to a large extent upon the yardstick used to measure it. In terms of the Soviet past much has been achieved; by Western standards the gains remain, by and large, unimpressive. It is a

THIS STOP, THE WINE & SPIRITS SHOP
NEXT STOP – THE END OF THE QUEUE

BUS STOPSKi

British cartoonist's depiction of a Soviet joke.

finally unanswerable question as to whether the security-oriented rights of the average Soviet citizen would have been better served by a capitalist state.

What has not been achieved in the Soviet Union is the removal of *privilege*, the right of the few to prosper at the expense of the many. Membership of the Soviet élite is only open to Communist Party members and to those who have contributed to Soviet power and prestige in some way such as through their artistic, scientific or sporting achievement. Members of the élite earn substantially larger salaries and, in addition, enjoy a range of benefits and privileges which are both a form of hidden income and a means of improving the quality of life. Membership of the elite – 'our Communist nobility' as one Soviet journalist dared to call it – brings with it such benefits as 'special' or 'closed' stores stocking luxury goods and non-luxury goods in chronically short supply in ordinary shops, special clinics and medical facilities, the right to a car and holiday and travel privileges.

Other forms of inequality in the provision of social and economic rights also exist in the USSR. Evidence from many sources suggests there is great disparity between urban and rural areas in fields such as education, health care, housing and welfare.

There are also inequalities between the sexes. The Soviet regime aims to remove sex discrimination and give women equal rights. Whilst much has been achieved – Soviet women enjoy one of the highest participation rates (86 per cent) in paid full-time employment – it is still the case that men dominate the positions of responsibility and authority.

All evidence – Soviet and Western – suggests, however, that spatial and gender inequalities in the USSR are decreasing. Bearing in mind the low and unequal level of development in the Soviet Union before the First World War, it is clear that great steps forward have been made in delivering security-oriented rights to the Soviet people but that there is still great room for improvement.

Two questions are central to any discussion of the human rights record of the Soviet Union. We have to ask whether Soviet denials of liberty-oriented rights have been bought at too high and unnecessary a price. Would security-oriented rights have been as well, if not better, achieved within a state offering civil and political liberties as much as securities? Or does the claim that *only through security is real liberty achieved* have substance? Even more central is the second question. Can the horrifying catalogue of basic rights violations – as described earlier in this chapter – ever be justified?

6 Indonesian expansionism: the case of East Timor

The invasion of East Timor

East Timor is the eastern half of an island lying 560 kilometres north of the coast of Australia. Colonised by the Portuguese in the late sixteenth century, it adjoins West Timor which formed part of the Dutch Empire until it became a province of the newly independent Republic of Indonesia in 1949.

The Republic of Indonesia has a population of about 153 million people and occupies a five-thousand kilometre arc of islands stretching from Sumatra in the west to Irian Jaya (West Papua) in the east. Rich in natural resources, including oil, it has been governed by a military dictatorship headed by General Suharto since 1965. The government has made a regular appearance on the 'gross violations' of human rights blacklist prepared annually by the United Nations Human Rights Commission. Tens of thousands of prisoners have been held without trial in Indonesian jails; torture is widespread and persistent; political and religious opposition to Suharto has been suppressed, newspapers and books banned, and trade unions crushed. In addition, Indonesia has shown herself to be intent upon territorial expansion. In 1962 West Papua was occupied. In December 1975 came the turn of East Timor.

Portugal's hold on East Timor began to loosen in April 1974 when the Portuguese dictator, Marcelo Caetano, was overthrown and a government came to power in Lisbon which was intent on giving

Indonesia and south-east Asia: East Timor was seized by Indonesia in 1975.

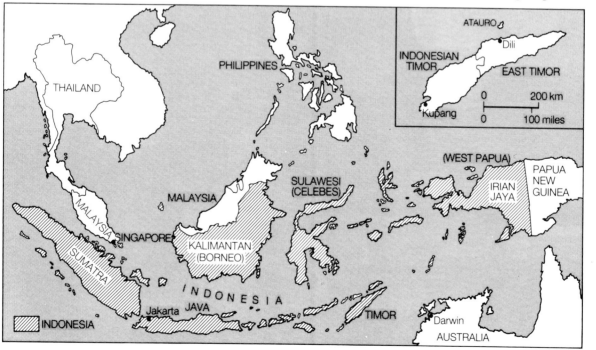

41

Statements of Adam Malik, Foreign Minister of Indonesia on East Timor

'The independence of every country is the right of every nation, with no exception for the people in Timor'
(17 June 1974)

'Independence is not an option for East Timor'
(4 December 1974)

'50,000 people or perhaps 80,000 people might have been killed during the war in East Timor... It was war... Then what is the big fuss?'
(30 March 1977)

Fretelin guerillas, 1983 (photograph smuggled out of East Timor).

Genocide
The act of deliberately killing a national, ethnic or racial group.

independence to its colonies. In East Timor rivalries between different Timorese political groups emerged, one group wanting to stay under Portuguese rule, one (the smallest group) calling for East Timor to become the twenty-seventh province of Indonesia, and a third favouring the establishment of an independent East Timor. A brief civil war broke out in August 1975 in which about 2,000 people were killed. The last mentioned group – 'Fretelin' – emerged victorious and immediately set about a programme of social and economic reform which quickly won the support of the majority of East Timorese. The period has been referred to by an independent observer as a 'temporary golden age' in East Timor's history. But the Indonesian regime, determined to prevent the emergence of an independent country on its border under a progressive government, launched armed invasions along the border from September to November. By 28 November the Indonesian military threat had become so serious that Fretelin decided to declare the establishment of the independent Democratic Republic of East Timor in order to be able to defend its territorial integrity at the United Nations.

A week later Indonesian forces mounted a full invasion. Paratroopers and marines took Dili, capital of East Timor, and quickly established a pattern of violent treatment of the people. On the day of the invasion journalists in Darwin, Australia, picked up a Fretelin Radio Dili Broadcast. 'The Indonesian forces are killing indiscriminately,' it alleged. 'Women and children are being shot in the streets. We are all going to be killed. I repeat, we are all going to be killed. This is an appeal for international help. Please do something to stop this invasion.' This broadcast was at first treated with some scepticism as a piece of Fretelin propaganda but, as the days and weeks passed, further evidence of wholesale Indonesian butchery filtered out of East Timor. Not only were Fretelin resistance-fighters being killed but also non-combatant Fretelin supporters and sympathisers, and other Timorese civilians. By February 1976 a pro-Indonesian East Timorese source was putting the number of those killed at 60,000.

As the Indonesian grip on East Timor tightened – a grip at first restricted to the main towns and to mainly lowland coastal villages on the road system – it became clear that the object of the military was to wipe out all support for Fretelin and for independence. The bloodshed continued as the invaders pushed into the interior mountain areas. Refugees arriving in Portugal told of 'excesses by Indonesian troops as they entered towns and villages'. Several prominent Timorese said that the killing in the inland mountain areas was far more extensive than it was in Dili, whole villages being wiped out as Indonesian troops advanced. An account was given of 'how Indonesians shot an entire family simply because they heard that the family had given a chicken to Fretelin soldiers; of families being shot when Indonesians discovered a Fretelin flag in their house'. An eyewitness reported that when Indonesian troops captured Remexio and Aileu all the villagers, except children under the age of three, were shot because they were infected by the seeds of Fretelin. A Catholic priest in East Timor described Indonesian policy as one of *genocide*. 'Consciences,' he wrote, 'are kept at peace by claiming that the people of Timor are "communists"...Even if they were communists, they would have the right to live.'

Prison conditions in Indonesian-controlled East Timor have been reported as appalling. Most of the prisoners are, in a loose sense,

A Fretelin political prisoner, Dominggas da Costa, arrested in 1982, tried in a show-trial and sentenced to six years imprisonment.

'political' detainees in that they have links with Fretelin or are relations or friends of Fretelin guerilla fighters. Evidence suggests that torture has been frequently administered on prisoners by their Indonesian jailers. Beatings and burnings with cigarettes appear commonplace.

The problem about using the word 'prison' with respect to Indonesian-occupied East Timor is that, in a sense, much of the country has been turned into a prison. To undermine remaining Fretelin resistance in the inland mountains, the villagers were first encouraged and then forced to move to 'resettlement centres' or 'strategic hamlets' usually in the coastal lowlands. By 1981 there were about 150 such centres. The Indonesian authorities justified the centres as making it easier 'to control the population and to provide food and medical aid, education and other amenities'. Most observers, however, have seen them as a denial of civil rights, aimed at isolating and starving out the Fretelin guerilla fighters in the mountains.

'Resettlement' also led to gross violations of the social and economic rights of the East Timorese. By forcing the people to leave their traditional mountain homes, a pattern of agriculture under which villages could be self-reliant was shattered. Corn and rice fields in the mountains reverted to nature and livestock died or went wild. In return, large numbers of people were forced to live in the 'resettlement centres' with insufficient land to meet their food needs. The resettlement policy of the Indonesians also overlooked the very good reasons why the majority of East Timorese chose to live in the mountains. In the lowlands malaria is endemic, water supplies poor, and the climate far hotter than in the highland areas. In short, resettlement has brought starvation, malnutrition and disease on a massive scale to East Timor. The former Bishop of Dili, forced to resign because of his outspoken condemnation of Indonesian brutality, said, 'If the people of East Timor could live where they liked, there would be no starvation in the country.'

In 1981 'Operation Security' was launched by the Indonesian army, its aim being to wipe out remaining Fretelin resistance. Every East Timorese male aged thirteen or above was ordered into the mountains to form a huge chain. Armed with sticks and crude weapons, they were forced up the mountains beating everything before them into a human

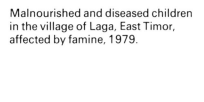

Malnourished and diseased children in the village of Laga, East Timor, affected by famine, 1979.

net. Hardly any Fretelin geurillas were caught as many of the conscripted Timorese let them slip through their legs or concealed them in their own midst. But many villagers were shot and thousands rounded up and sent to Atauro prison island. 'Operation Security' caused further widespread devastation, in that the men were in the mountains when they should have been planting the food crops in time for the rainy season. The result was a disastrous harvest in 1982 and a further wave of famine.

Estimates as to how many East Timorese died in the five years after December 1975 vary widely. The last Portuguese census was in 1970 and arrived at a population of 610,541. Assuming a 2 per cent annual growth rate in population, there would have been at least 650,000 East Timorese by December 1975. An official Indonesian census in December 1980 put the population at 552,954. If that figure is accepted, then at least 15 per cent of the population died between 1975 and 1980. Other sources outside Indonesia put the number of deaths as high as 200,000 (in other words, almost one third of the estimated 1975 population).

'Selective indignation' about human rights

'East Timor? Where's that?', might be a typical response if the subject was brought up in conversation. Yet the tragedy of East Timor has had few equals in the twentieth century. How can it happen that we remain so ignorant of such a horrifying present-day tale of genocide?

East Timor has been a victim of the 'selective indignation' which affects international human rights politics. While Western governments have been vocal in their criticism of the rights record of some countries, they have, for the most part, chosen to turn a blind eye to what has happened in East Timor because of Indonesia's economic and strategic importance. Described by President Nixon of the USA as 'the greatest prize in the south-east Asia area', Indonesia is a major raw materials producer and exporter to the West (including Australia, New Zealand and Japan). The West needs Indonesian oil. In addition, the Suharto government is strongly anti-Communist and is seen as an important buffer against Communist expansion in the region. A Fretelin-led East Timor, it was felt, might become pro-Communist. It was for these reasons that the US government refused to support East Timorese independence. 'Such a policy,' it was stated, 'would not serve our best interests in the light of the importance of our relations with Indonesia.'

Such considerations explain why the US and most other Western governments did nothing to ensure that UN Security Council Resolutions calling for Indonesian withdrawal from East Timor were implemented (Security Council Resolutions are binding on UN members). They also help to explain why the West has continued to sell arms to Indonesia. The United States has been the major supplier of arms – even under President Carter who, we have noted in Chapter 2, proclaimed human rights to be the yardstick of his foreign policy. In 1978 the British Labour Government approved the sale of eight BAC Hawk ground attack aircraft to Indonesia (worth about £25,000,000). Such aircraft are particularly suited for East Timorese combat conditions with their ability to fly low and to drop napalm and

Export boom in arms for Indonesia

A NEW ROUND of arms sales to Indonesia is planned by British government officials, according to a classified report obtained by the *New Statesman*. The report reveals that the Department of Trade is planning to raise Indonesia's creditworthiness for export guarantees to at least £1 billion this year and £2 billion overall. Of this, £340 million would go for arms sales.

The Conservative government's attitude to Indonesia, which almost seven years ago invaded the former Portuguese colony of East Timor, is in distinct contrast to the stance taken against invading Argentina this year, when ministers successfully won the arms and trade embargoes against Argentina. More than 100,000 of the inhabitants of East Timor are believed to have died during the Indonesian repression. In indonesia up to a million leftists and others are estimated to have died since the dictatorship of President Soeharto was established in 1965.

According to a paper prepared by the Country Policy Division of the Export Credits Guarantee Department two months ago, an official visit to Indonesia in February by Lord Carrington and an entourage of businessmen was successful in drumming up arms business — all related directly to the continued repression in East Timor. The items they hope to sell are

- A Mark 15 Frigate, worth £273.3 million, and possibly Type 21 Frigates
- Five British Aerospace Hawk aircraft, worth £29 million
- Eleven Armoured Security Vehicles, worth £1.2 million
- Sea Wolf missile launchers, worth £36 million in cash.

It is a safe sale because, as the document notes, there is in Indonesia 'No effective challenge to the present system of government . . . the existing regime is unlikely to change.'

This week, the United Nations is voting on self-determination for East Timor, on which this government has always abstained. Liberal peer Lord Avebury told the United Nations this week that Britain was guilty of 'complicity and acquiescence' in Indonesian repression. As the task force sailed against Argentian repression in May, *Tapol*, the British Committee for the Defence of Political Prisoners and Human Rights in Indonesia, wrote to the Foreign Office to ask for an arms embargo against Indonesia too. Mr Richard Powell, of the South-East Asia Department of the FO, wrote back that the 'important differences' were that the Falkland Islands were under 'British Administration' and were 'inhabited by people of predominantly British stock'. East Timor, he wrote, was 'quite different'.

Duncan Campbell

Article by Duncan Campbell from the *New Statesman*, 18 November 1982.

defoliants in anti-guerilla warfare. Further arms sales were being negotiated by the British Conservative Government in 1983.

In other words, Western nations have felt it to be in their interest to say little about atrocities and human rights violations in East Timor. With a few notable exceptions, Western press, radio and television have gone along with their governments by reporting virtually nothing. The average person in the West knows little, if anything, about East Timor because in international relations it is convenient to be concerned about some human rights violations but very inconvenient to be concerned about others. 'Selective indignation' is a world-wide phenomenon. Amnesty International and other human rights groups strongly criticised the British government for making so much of human rights violations in Argentina during the Falklands War when it had virtually ignored those violations prior to the break-out of hostilities with Argentina. The Soviet press regularly condemns Western support of South Africa, Indonesia and the South American military regimes while turning a blind eye to gross rights violations in areas under Soviet control or influence such as Afghanistan, Ethiopia and South Yemen.

7 Human rights in the West

In the last three chapters we have examined human rights denials and violations in Communist and Third World countries far removed from Western democracies. It would be both wrong and dangerous to leave the story there and so imply that we in the West have a 'clean' human rights record; that violations occur 'out there' but not 'at home'. This chapter will show that there is no room for smugness or self-congratulation on our part about human rights.

'Dam a river, damn a people': the Sami of Lapland

Norway has long prided itself on its human rights record. At the United Nations it has been at the forefront in defending the rights of the oppressed black population of South Africa and in condemning the bestial treatment of prisoners by certain Latin-American governments. It was an early signatory of the European Convention on Human Rights and Norwegians were quick to become active in Amnesty International when it was established in 1961 (see Chapters 9 and 10). It is more generous in its aid to Third World countries than most other Western democracies.

The Sami people – the Lapps – inhabit the northern part of Norway, Sweden and Finland and the north-western tip of the Soviet Union.

Sami-inhabited areas in northern Europe.

Lassoing yearlings prior to the trek from winter to spring pastures: skill with the lasso is vital for the successful herder. This herding unit is in Finnmark country – a unit whose area was infringed upon by the 'Alta–Kautokeino Hydro-electric Project'.

Sami tent, or *lavvo*: although herders also own modern houses, the *lavvo* is highly functional, used for herding all the year round, and has become a symbol of Sami unity and resistance.

A *ski-doo,* or motorised sledge, with a well-trained dog behind: mobility is basic to herding, and the Sami use modern technology alongside traditional methods, to obtain greater control over their herds.

Many live in the tundra region where the vegetation is low-lying; the climate is harsh and the region unable to support a large human population. Out of a total population of 549,000 in northern Norway only an estimated 25,000 are Sami. Even in their own region, therefore, they are a minority. Their way of life, which has traditionally been dependent upon reindeer herding, salmon fishing and small-scale agriculture, means that their numbers are spread thinly over a large area rather than being concentrated in a few small regions. It has been Sami practice and tradition to live in close harmony with – and never to exploit – their environment. The preservation of the environment is essential to the preservation of their way of life.

In recent times, however, the environment of northern Norway has been put under increasing pressure. The last two decades have seen a tremendous growth in tourism; fishing, hiking, shooting and skiing have begun to take their toll of the natural resources upon which the Sami rely. Norway is part of NATO, the Western defence system, and the government has reserved large areas of 'wilderness' for military training by the Western allies. In addition, timber-felling continues to destroy forest (reindeer feed on lichen off the trees) to meet the demands of the Norwegian paper industry.

Each of these three factors has helped to undermine the Sami way of life. The most controversial development, however, has been the Norwegian government's determination to push ahead with a programme of hydro-electric projects to meet the energy requirements of Oslo and the more heavily populated industrial areas of southern Norway. Norwegians enjoy one of the highest standards of living in the 'rich North'; they use more energy per person than almost anyone else in the world. Over the last thirty years more than a hundred rivers in northern Norway have been dammed, flooding huge tracts of land to meet the demand for energy.

Each dam built in a Sami area threatens their livelihood. The dams put an end to salmon migration up the river and its tributaries for breeding purposes. Some of the best grazing, mating and calving areas for reindeer herds have been submerged under artificial lakes and reservoirs. Road construction to the dams interferes with reindeer migration (as do new roads built for tourism). Sami freedom of movement has been curtailed as the irregular flow of water prevents rivers from freezing so they cannot be crossed in winter.

The final straw for the Sami was a government announcement in 1970 that a large dam and hydro-electric scheme was to be built at Masi on the banks of the river Alta in the heart of Sami reindeer country. Prior to the announcement, there had been no consultation with the Sami people or their representatives. There was intense opposition to the scheme from NSR, the Sami organisation, and from local communes. This delayed the start of the project and led the government to somewhat reduce the size of the dam. Nonetheless, the Norwegian Parliament approved the scheme in 1978 and work on approach roads to the dam commenced.

The reaction on the part of some Sami was to engage in a campaign of passive resistance. Three times between 1979 and 1981, Sami sat across the approach road and chained themselves to the giant earth-moving machines and trucks. On the second occasion in January 1981 they were joined by other local people and by sympathisers from all over Norway. Nine hundred people were confronted by six hundred police; many demonstrators were arrested and heavily fined. Perhaps because of the heavy fines, the passive resistance campaign ended in

'We came first'; 'We don't move': placards in the Sami demonstration protesting against the plans to flood Masi, which greeted a parliamentary committee in 1970. Masi, a small Sami community of about four hundred inhabitants, fiercely opposed plans for the hydro-electric project, which suggested that the whole community was to be flooded.

1981 and work on the dam began. The campaign did achieve something, however. The Alta River confrontation brought the plight of the Sami to the attention of the Norwegian public. As a result, a Parliamentary Commission on Sami Rights was set up in 1980.

The case of the Sami raises a number of important human rights questions. Article 17 of the Universal Declaration states that 'no one shall be arbitrarily deprived of his property'. Yet what constitutes 'property' in the case of indigenous people, reliant upon fishing and the herding and hunting of wild animals? Interestingly, a treaty of 1751 between Norway and Sweden gave the Sami freedom of movement and the right to use the land and water as a means of subsistence for themselves and their animals. Article 23 of the Universal Declaration calls for 'free choice of employment' and 'just and favourable conditions of work'. Are the conditions of work for the Sami in their chosen and traditional employment – the very basis of their culture – being undermined to the extent that a rights' denial is involved? Then there is the wider question of whether and to what extent the demands of the Norwegian *majority* for more and more energy, for as high as possible a standard of living, should be permitted to override the interests of the Sami *minority*. On the other hand, should the Sami have some right of veto over the manner of how their lands are exploited? If so, at what point would that right become an unacceptable private property right? The Alta River confrontation has also been seen by some Norwegians as a landmark in the 'struggle against the consumer values of their affluent country'. The case of the Sami raises in miniature a central and very uncomfortable question for the people of the industrialised world. If they are indeed committed to the promotion of human rights, ought they to curtail their pursuit of affluence and, thus, release precious resources for the benefit of those living 'beyond the pale' of affluent industrialised society?

Whose land? The Aborigines of Australia

The land rights issue

● Aborigines still living in a traditional way want to be granted freehold title over their ancestral lands. In the Northern Territory and South Australia, Aborigines now own, freehold, large areas of their homelands. In New South Wales and Victoria, the much smaller reserves have also been returned to Aboriginal ownership. But Queensland, Tasmania and Western Australia have not followed suit.

● Aborigines who no longer have a close connection with their traditional lands want a grant of land on which they can build a future, and secure their social and economic needs.

● Aborigines claim land in the name of justice, as compensation for being dispossessed of their traditional lands.

● They believe that lands claims are inextricably linked with Aboriginal religious beliefs: without land cultural identity is destroyed.

Recording an interview for Australia's first Aboriginal radio station, which has been broadcasting from Alice Springs, Northern Territory since 1985, reaching both black and white communities.

Since the 1960s the Aborigines have been prominent on the Australian political scene. The 'Land Rights Movement' has featured as central to their struggle. Most Aborigines see the return of their ancestral land and the right to own and manage the reserves (some of which are still effectively controlled by white managers) as a vital step towards self-determination. For the Aborigines living on and off reserves, for those now living in cities, and for the thousands still leading a traditional life style in the bush, the movement has also become a symbolic rallying point for all the historic grievances of the Aborigines against their white compatriots.

The Aborigines' civilisation spans over 40,000 years. They evolved a way of life which balanced their needs with the country's fragile ecosystem – they had few material possessions and they moved around, hunting and gathering. Traditionally Aboriginal culture is governed by a deep, spiritual affinity with the land – a spirit derived from the sacredness of the Dreaming. If Aborigines are dispossessed of their land, they are dispossessed of their spirit, their reason for being. Aboriginal spokesman, Silas Roberts writes, 'I have met many Aborigines who have lost their land, and by losing their land they have lost a part of themselves. By way of example they are like Christians who have lost their soul, and don't know where they are – just wandering.'

For the British colonists, however, the land was 'discovered'. It was regarded as *terra nullius* (empty land), the settlers' view being that it wasn't really 'owned'. Australia formally became a British colony in 1788: the colonists claimed that they were in effect settling Australia for the first time and so could introduce the British system of law. Aborigines maintain, however, that they did own Australia, that it was taken from them by force of arms. They argue that there has never been a negotiated treaty, and many whites support them today in their fight for a negotiated settlement.

Thus began the destruction of the Aborigines and their way of life, reinforced by a strong contempt for a 'primitive' people. Sacred sites were desecrated, they were dispossessed of their land, and entire tribes were exterminated. In the early twentieth century Aborigines were forcibly settled on State reserves, subject to racist laws and harassment. Up to the 1950s, 'abo-hunting' was a recognised sport in the outback. Even today, petty laws still regulate Aborigines on the reserves which they do not yet own.

Having promised to take up the cause of land rights in 1983, the Australian Federal Labor government was forced to back down by the powerful influence of cattle and mining interests and the resistance of individual States to Federal government. A few Aborigines have now been elected to the Federal and State parliaments, and Aborigines manage their own Development Commission and many legal, health, housing and sporting bodies, all publicly funded. Nevertheless, despite these developments, the concept of *terra nullius* remains enshrined in Australian law and life.

1 Bauxite (raw aluminium) – Eastern Arnhem Land (1968) deposits on largest Aboriginal reserve in State, exploited by holding company owned by Alusuisse (Switzerland). Small royalty payments negotiated with Aborigines as compensation. Severe water pollution from local refinery affects local people. Stripmining (i.e. removing topsoil to excavate shallow-lying deposits: cheapest and most destructive mining method – leaving a lunar landscape of rock rubble, destroying vegetation and animal life).

2 Bauxite – Weipa and Mapoon (1957) world's largest known deposit of bauxite. Lease to mine 1,600 square kilometres owned by Rio Tinto Zinc (UK) and Kaiser Aluminium (USA). Mine covers much of reserve. Compensation to Aborigines: construction of 62 houses.

3 Diamonds – Oombulgurri (1976) exploration rights granted to consortium including Rio Tinto Zinc (UK), De Beers (South Africa) and Broken Hill Pty (Australia). Federal government refused mining operations in 1977 in order to protect Aborigine rights. State government overruled refusal. No Aboriginal compensation.

4 Uranium – Western Arnhem Land (1978) one of the world's largest deposits. Major companies involved include Getty Oil (USA), Peko Wallsend (Australia), Noranda (Canada) and the Australian Atomic Energy Commission. Sustained opposition to mining since 1978. Disputed and controversial settlement in 1978 by the Aboriginal Northern Land Council on two sites, with 4½% royalties as compensation.

The mining conflict

Northern Territory
Western Australia
South Australia
Queensland
New South Wales
Victoria
Tasmania
Darwin
Perth
Brisbane
Adelaide
Sydney
Melbourne
Hobart

Aboriginal reserves and Land Trust Areas (LTA) (shown to scale)

• Reserves and LTA too small to show to scale

+ Location of mining (details of mineral exploitation in key, including geographical location, and year of major decision on the go-ahead)

The discovery of valuable mineral resources in the Australian outback in the 1960s made the question of land rights even more acute. Nominally the rights to minerals on Aboriginal Reserves rests with the Federal government in Canberra. But the real authority for who mines what and where, does, in general, rest with the State governments, which receive royalties from the mining companies. Aborigines who have been given their land do have considerable control over the mining development on it. They may refuse any development, or negotiate for royalties and agreements. But ultimately, 'in the national interest' as defined by government, they have to permit mining in particular cases. In general, Aborigines are often prepared to allow mining on parts of their land which are not sacred, provided they can negotiate for acceptable conditions. The resulting income gives them a chance to develop their lives in ways which are independent of government and the dominant white society.

WE DON'T WANT LAND RIGHTS WE WANT AN EQUAL WAY OF LIFE FOR ALL AUSTRALIANS

While Aborigines continue to fight for rights to land which had been lived on by countless generations of their ancestors, certain white interests have been claiming rights of a different sort – the rights of the majority. White opposition in Queensland, Western Australia, and other States argue that:

● Aborigines are being treated differentially in that they are given land, whereas white groups are not.

● Giving Aborigines land will create a 'separate nation' in Australia and will lead to a kind of 'apartheid' in reverse.

● Giving Aborigines control over land will prevent the exploitation of natural resources and access to terrains (national parks etc.) which belong to the Australian people as a whole, both black and white.

Teacher left jobless

Gerhard von Schnehen

Gerhard was sacked in March 1983 for speaking out against neo-fascism at a school in Goslar, Lower Saxony. But he has been told that he was "not defending the free democratic order". In other words, he was an enemy of the state.

Since 1982 there have been 800 similar cases in Lower Saxony alone.

All are victims of Berufsverbot, the campaign against people employed in the public sector who have left wing views.

Gerhard's "crime" was to write to a local newspaper expressing his approval of a court decision to sentence another teacher who had told pupils that the holocaust never took place, that photographs of dead Jews had been faked by the Americans and that Hitler planned to make Palestine a Jewish homeland.

The authorities had two other complaints. Firstly he had written a letter to his trade union journal criticising the deployment of Cruise missiles and secondly he had donated money to the Communist Party. When his probation ended he was sacked.

His dismissal flew in the face of advice from the education department which could find no fault with his teaching of English, history and social science at an 11 to 16 middle school in Goslar.

A glimpse of West Germany: the *Berufsverbot*

Like most other Western democracies, West Germany witnessed a period of youth and student protest in the late 1960s. Marches, demonstrations and sit-ins were frequent as young people took up radical political causes. By 1970 the West German government was becoming nervous as those same young people finished their studies and began to enter professional life. A decree was issued in 1972 introducing the *Berufsverbot*, or profession ban. The *Berufsverbot* forbids the employment in the public services of individuals if their loyalty to the democratic basis of society is considered to be in any way in doubt. Security checks are enforced on those suspected of disloyalty or 'extremism'. The screening covers those already in jobs as well as those seeking public employment. In West Germany some 20 per cent of all workers are in what are regarded as public service jobs (the term 'public' or 'civil' servant includes teachers, clergymen, some state-industry workers as well as those working for government departments). Those having 'extreme' political views have been screened as have their friends and acquaintances. By 1978 over a million security checks on individuals had been carried out and approximately 10,000 had been denied or dismissed from a job.

In theory such checks apply to individuals on both left and right of the political spectrum. In practice, *Berufsverbot* has most often been applied against the left. Indeed, the neo-Nazi National Democratic Party was cleared in 1978 of having aims and policies hostile to the West German constitution.

The *Berufsverbot* raises serious questions about a leading democratic country which claims to be firmly committed to the pursuance of human rights.

Article 19 of the Universal Declaration asserts that 'everyone has the right to freedom of opinion and expression; this right includes freedom to hold opinions without interference'. Article 23 lays down the right to work and to free choice of employment. If a situation exists in which individuals can only take up or continue in employment if their political opinions are acceptable to the state, are these rights infringed? If so, can such infringements be justified on the grounds that the state has the right to protect itself from subversives (people attempting to undermine the state)? How far should a democratic society tolerate those who are believed to want to work to overthrow it and replace it with an undemocratic society? Also, when is a person a subversive and when is he or she simply exercising freedom of opinion (see the case of Gerhard von Schnehen)? Do democratic, communist and totalitarian regimes have an equal right to protect themselves against what they regard as subversion?

'It's a free country': human rights in Great Britain

'It couldn't happen here. It's a free country.' It is often claimed that Britain leads the world in championing civil and political liberties; that Britain is a tolerant country, respectful of equal rights and its people as alert as ever to any signs of growth in state control over their lives. Let us examine some aspects of the recent record.

First, privacy. Article 12 of the Universal Declaration reads as follows:

No one shall be subjected to arbitrary interference with his privacy, family, home or correspondence, nor to attacks upon his honour and reputation. Everyone has the right to the protection of law against such interference or attacks.

Mr Moses Edwards of Talysarn, North Wales, might read these lines a little ruefully given what happened on 6 January 1982. While making a telephone call from the village telephone box, Mr Edwards discovered a device the size of a pocket radio which was snatched from him by two men who then drove away. The local police later admitted planting a bugging device in the booth but gave no reason why they had done so (journalists guessed that it was part of the investigation into arson attacks on empty holiday cottages in Wales). The incident created concern amongst civil rights lawyers, especially when the existence of secret Home Office guidelines on telephone surveillance was revealed. The police do not require *warrants* for the planting of bugging devices as they do for telephone tapping and for opening of letters (although the approval of the Chief Constable in question is required).

A 1980 Government White Paper stated that 467 phone-tapping warrants and 52 mail-interception warrants were issued in 1979. These figures must be treated rather sceptically. They did not include the regular interception of all overseas telegrams and telephone calls by the Government Communications Headquarters or the tapping of diplomatic calls. The White Paper also admitted that a warrant could be issued against a 'target' organisation, individual or activity and might, therefore, cover the tapping of many telephone lines. Ominously, it revealed that the Home Secretary had extended the scope of telephone tapping to cover not only security matters and serious offences but also 'lesser' offences where violence *might* occur. Such a loose definition opened the prospect of telephone tapping being authorised in, for instance, the case of people planning a demonstration, or in the case of trade unionists planning to picket a factory.

In August 1984 the European Court of Human Rights (see Chapter 9) judged that the system of interception of communications in Britain violated the right to privacy. The system was particularly criticised because it was based on Home Office warrants and not on statute law. As a result the government hurried through the Interception of Communications Act in 1985 (which came into effect in April 1986), taking the existing warranty system and giving it parliamentary authority. A judicial tribunal was also established so that people could appeal if they suspected that their mail was being intercepted or telephone tapped unlawfully (i.e. without warrant). If the tribunal finds that an interception has occurred without warrant, the subject is compensated. On the other hand, the subject may be informed by the tribunal that 'no violation has taken place'. This could mean that the person's mail has not been intercepted, nor the telephone tapped, or it could mean that one or more interceptions have taken place but were based on the issue of a warrant (and thus not illegal). The subject is not told by the tribunal which alternative applies. What is not certain from the act is whether the tribunal has the authority to investigate the evidence behind the Home Office's decision to issue a warrant, and, hence, to make a judgement on that decision. Civil rights groups are watching this anxiously in that if the tribunal cannot investigate and judge the validity of warrants then the machinery set up under the act could prove to be an elaborate means of stonewalling citizens' complaints.

Warrant
A writ giving the police authority to arrest a person or to carry out an act such as a search.

MI5 — THIS CONTAINS FILES ON EVERYONE WHO'S SPOKEN OUT IN FAVOUR OF A FREEDOM OF INFORMATION ACT

TOP SECRET

Examples of organisations – both government and private – which hold records on citizens in Britain: much information is on computer, and could be linked together to provide a very detailed picture of an individual's daily life.

As in other technologically advanced countries, the right to privacy in Britain is also increasingly threatened by the growth of an immense data-collection network. The Police National Computer (PNC) at Hendon in London carries over thirty million records on individuals and is linked to most police stations in the country by Visual Display Units (VDUs). In 1979 the PNC was said to be dealing with 160,000 enquiries a day. The PNC carried records of vehicle ownership (which are transferred automatically and without the owner's consent from the Vehicle Licensing Centre), stolen vehicles, fingerprints, disqualified drivers, wanted and missing persons and an index of criminal records. Such records seem harmless enough but disturbing facts have come to light. Evidence has emerged, for instance, that vehicle records sometimes refer to the political organisations to which a person belongs. PNC is also vulnerable to use by people outside the police force. In 1976 *The Times* reported that people had obtained information from PNC over the telephone by posing as police officers.

- **MI5** (Government secret security service) can request virtually any computer information from the police, Immigration, Office of Population, Censuses and Surveys, DHSS, Department of Employment, Inland Revenue, British Telecom, banks, credit cards or any of the 200 'data bases' in government hands. MI5 keep extensive records of known political activists.

- **THE POLICE** can obtain information from the Post Office, British Telecom, Immigration, banks, DVLC, Gas and Electricity Boards, etc. The police increasingly use computers: there is the Police National Computer at Hendon, which stores criminal records, as well as over 53 million personal records, the vast majority of which have nothing to do with criminal activities. Police cameras are now used to read car number-plates on key routes; roof-top video cameras can record demonstrations.

- **INLAND REVENUE** keep much information on computer and have very detailed personal files on every taxpayer. They have wide powers of search and seizure.

- **CUSTOMS & EXCISE** keep details and records of any VAT-registered business and those exporting and importing goods.

- **DEPARTMENT OF EMPLOYMENT** holds computerised records for unemployment benefits.

- **BRITISH TELECOM** Besides making phone-tapping easier, new micro-chip telephone exchanges are capable of providing itemised computerised bills showing the numbers called and duration of calls.

- **POST OFFICE** provides a mail interception service for the police.

- **GAS AND ELECTRICITY BOARDS** now do accounts by computer. Such information can reveal changing patterns in a house – showing when it's in use and when not, and how many people are likely to be living there.

- **BANKS** have discretion as to when to release details of transactions. If banks refuse, various Government agencies can obtain a court order for statements etc. to be turned over to them. Legal judgements indicate that this should be done only when a 'higher public interest' than the privacy of the indivdual is involved.

- **CREDIT AND CHARGE CARDS** Both types of card can provide vivid diary-like details of an individual's financial transactions.

- **DHSS DEPARTMENT OF HEALTH AND SOCIAL SECURITY** Much social security information is kept on computer. There is also an increasing trend to computerise medical records which could include sensitive information on abortions, venereal diseases etc.

- **DRIVER VEHICLE LICENSING CENTRE (DVLC)** can provide computerised details of cars, owners and addresses to police in seconds.

- **OFFICE OF POPULATION, CENSUSES AND SURVEYS** The census reveals personal details of household occupancy and much of this data is computerised.

- **IMMIGRATION** 'Machine-readable passports' are planned to be introduced throughout Europe. Immigration offices would simply have to slip your passport into a machine which would read coded electronic information invisible to the passport's owner. Linked into other computers, this will give an instantaneous permanent record of the individual's travels throughout Europe, and contain information about, for example, alleged political activities.

1984 Data Protection Act

Under this act, it is a criminal offence to keep computer records about a person unless the data base is registered with the Data Protection Register.

Individuals (from November 1987) will have the right to see and challenge information about themselves. (This includes the right of access of students to any computer-stored school records, including exam marks.)

However, civil liberties campaigners argue that:

● The act does not cover manual records, so damaging material could be transferred to paper

● The act does not allow data-subjects to correct inaccurate data; they may, with difficulty, apply to a court for the data to be expunged from a record

● The act does not allow government departments to be prosecuted for any offence; only private users may be prosecuted

● There is no supervision or inspection of data-users after registration; violations of the act will usually only be detected if the data-subject happens to stumble across evidence of abuse

● The act provides no safeguard against a data-subject being forced to obtain access to sensitive personal data about themselves, and then to pass it on to a third party (such as an interviewee being asked to produce a copy of their criminal record)

Sex discrimination

Treating a woman less favourably than a man because of her sex or treating a man less favourably than a woman because of his sex.

Job segregation

Separating people as regards the type of job they do, perhaps on grounds of race or sex.

A real danger for the future privacy of the citizen lies in any linking up of the different computers that already collect gigantic amounts of data on people's daily lives. The power of the state to survey the private life of the individual would be enormously increased if the 200 or so government-controlled 'data bases' already functioning were plugged together to make a complete national system which also included business, bank, credit card and other commercial computers.

Britain has lagged behind many other Western democracies in protecting the citizen against the collection and use of personal information, computerised and non-computerised. Privacy or Data Protection Acts were, for instance, passed in Sweden (1973), in the USA (1974) and in France and West Germany (1978).

From 1967 onwards a number of Data Protection Bills were put before the British Parliament but it was not until 1984 that a Data Protection Act was passed. The act made it a criminal offence to keep computer records about a person unless the data base was registered with the Data Protection Register. Companies and other institutions having a data base were given six months from 1985 to register, whilst subjects' right of access to data about themselves could be exercised under the act from November 1987. The act was passed partly in response to pressure from civil rights campaigners, but it had also been strongly urged by businesspeople and scientists, since countries with data protection laws were not allowing their businesses and organisations to transfer information to British computers until privacy was equally protected in Britain. Civil rights organisations have been critical of the act in that it applies only to computer data bases although ninety per cent of data is kept in manual form. The act, they argue, encourages the keeping of manual records so as to sidestep the law. It is a moot point, they add, as to whether manual records with computerised indexes are covered by the legislation. Finally, they are concerned about data bases that are exempted under the act, in particular the exemption of agencies of government with regard to national security (widely defined).

The Universal Declaration of Human Rights insists that women should share equal rights with men and should receive equal pay for equal work. Although Britain signed the Declaration in 1948, it was 1975 before two Acts of Parliament came into effect protecting the rights of women and guaranteeing equal pay. The *Equal Pay Act* of 1970 – which came into effect in 1975 – made it unlawful to pay a woman less for doing broadly similar work to a man. The *Sex Discrimination Act* of 1975 made it unlawful to discriminate on grounds of sex in education, training, employment and the provision of goods, facilities and services.

The above two laws notwithstanding, civil liberties campaigners remain critical of the British record in protecting women's rights. In 1970, when the Equal Pay Act was passed, women's average earnings were 63.1 per cent of men's. By 1977 the gap had narrowed to 73.5 per cent. Unless there is new legislation, it is not likely to close much further. The crucial point is that *job segregation* has become part of British working life; women tend to be concentrated in a few areas of the job market such as catering and secretarial work. Because these areas of work are women-dominated and are not jobs done by men, the Equal Pay Act fails to help women. It is also the case that half the women workers in Britain are in part-time jobs for which there is inadequate legal protection. The Sex Discrimination Act also fails to give equal rights to women in pension, social security and taxation matters.

Cook wins right to equal pay with craftsmen in shipyard

Canteen cook Julie Hayward has won the right to equal pay with a painter, joiner and thermal heating engineer in the same shipyard, after a ruling by a Liverpool Industrial Tribunal that her work is of equal value to theirs.

Her case is the first successful one to be brought under the amendments to the equal pay legislation, introduced in January 1984.

Until the amendments were introduced, to bring Britain into line with European legislation, it had in many cases been difficult for women to obtain comparable levels of pay with men. One of the reasons for this is that women tend to be segregated into "women's" jobs, usually the lowest paid and with the lowest levels of responsibility and there are no men doing such work with whom the women could compare themselves for equal pay purposes. It is noteworthy that women's earnings stand at around 74 per cent of men's.

The Equal Pay Act originally allowed a woman to claim equal pay only where she was doing the same or broadly similar work to a man or where there had been a job evaluation study, which had given her job the same value as that of a man in each case in the same employment.

Under the amendments, a woman can now in addition compare her work with that of a man of equal value to his, even though the jobs are not the same or broadly similar and have not been evaluated under a job evaluation study.

The Tribunal held that her work at Cammell Laird, Shipbuilders, on Merseyside, for which she received £99 a week, was of equal value and demanded the same skill, knowledge and responsibility as the jobs of the men in the shipyard who were paid £130 a week as painters, joiners and thermal engineers.

She was required to undertake the same length of training as other craft apprentices and for three of the four year apprenticeship was paid at the same rate as her trainee male colleagues. But when she qualified as a canteen assistant she was paid less than they were.

The Tribunal ruling is a great step forward for women, who now, under the amendments to the Equal Pay Act, do not necessarily have to find a man doing the same, or broadly similar work, in the same workplace, to compare themselves with, in order to claim equal pay.

Article from *Equality Now!*, Winter 1985.

Racial discrimination
Treating a person of one race less favourably than a person of a different race.

Similarly, the *Race Relations Acts* of 1965, 1968 and 1976, outlawing racial discrimination, have failed to ensure full and equal rights for members of Britain's racial minorities. The reasons for this are many but British law and practice over immigration has contributed to the threat and insecurity felt by black communities. The effect of the Immigration Act of 1971 and subsequent Immigration Rules has virtually been to create two classes of immigrant into Britain. Millions of white Commonwealth citizens from countries such as Australia and Canada can enter and work in Britain freely as long as they have one grandparent who was born in Britain. Similarly, under EEC rules, the 200 million mainly white citizens of the Common Market can enter Britain for six months and are free to stay if they obtain work. On the other hand, non-whites from the New Commonwealth (Africa, Asia and the Caribbean) face a tangled web of immigration restrictions even though they possess British passports.

One question that needs to be faced is how Britain's immigration regulations square with her acceptance of Article 2 of the Universal Declaration, under which all rights are to be enjoyed irrespective of race or colour.

The effect of the immigration restrictions on people from the New Commonwealth has been to keep husbands and wives and members of the same family apart from each other. There have been well-documented cases of children being delayed or refused permission to join their parents in Britain, of elderly parents being refused admission to join sons or daughters, of married people being refused admission to join their spouses and of fiancés and fiancées being prevented from joining their intended partners in marriage. In recalling such cases, we should not lose sight of the fact that the British government is a signatory of the Universal Declaration which lays down the right to marry 'without limitation due to race, nationality or religion' and which states that 'the family is the natural and fundamental group unit of society and is entitled to protection by society and the State'. The European Convention on Human Rights, likewise, protects the right to marry and have a family life. In 1982 a group of women, kept separate from their foreign husbands under British Immigration Rules, took their complaints to the European

Commission of Human Rights. In 1985, the European Court judged that certain articles of the Convention had been violated, and that the women had been discriminated against on the grounds of sex. The British government, obliged to abide by the judgement, has now brought its Immigration Rules into line with those of the Convention.

The examples given in this chapter serve to illustrate that the denials and violations of human rights that occur in countries like Norway, Australia, West Germany and Britain are both different in scale and degree to those described in earlier chapters. In Norway one can write and protest on behalf of the Sami people without much fear of imprisonment; in Britain one can write a book like this without fear of assassination or disappearance or without risk of being forcibly detained in a psychiatric hospital.

In most but not all cases, rights denials and violations can be exposed and pursued. The governments of Norway, West Germany and Britain are accountable to a democratic process – however imperfect – and are prepared to allow individuals to take cases to the European Commission and Court of Human Rights. They have also undertaken to remedy the situation if the Commission or Court judges a rights denial to have occurred (see Chapter 9).

These examples offer sufficient indication, however, that human rights should not be taken for granted in democratic societies. Growing international tensions, declining economic growth and rising unemployment lead to growing tensions within society. As dissent and protest increase, the danger increases that those in positions of power will become less scrupulous in their respect for human rights.

The 1980s have witnessed a continued upward trend in the number of rights violations complaints against the British government put before the European Commission of Human Rights. This has led a growing body of politicians and lawyers to call for a new Bill of Rights to be enacted by parliament. It is often pointed out that some three centuries have passed since Britain's last Bill of Rights (1689) and that Western countries such as West Germany and the USA have basic rights laws to protect citizens' freedom. Many supporters of the idea think that a Bill of Rights could be created by incorporating the European Convention on Human Rights (see Chapter 9) into British law. Other supporters think that the European Convention does not go far enough as it does not include social and economic rights. Opponents of the idea argue that a Bill of Rights would give too much power to the judges and tie the hands of subsequent parliaments, in that a Bill would only be worth enacting if it were powerful enough to invalidate future laws that violated its contents. In other words, a later expression of democratic will would be overturned by *entrenched* legislation passed earlier.

PART THREE   THE DEFENCE OF HUMAN RIGHTS

8   The United Nations and human rights

Theo van Boven.

The sacking of Theo van Boven

Early in 1982, Theo van Boven, the Dutch Director of the United Nations Human Rights Commission, was sacked for making a speech in which, in plain language, he accused seven governments of carrying out arbitrary killings of their citizens.

Theo van Boven had taken up office in 1977. His vigorous pursuance of human rights won him more enemies than friends. Latin-American governments were angrily defensive about the United Nations probe into disappearances which he had been responsible for establishing; the US government was uneasy about his exposing human rights violations in Latin American states friendly to US interests; the Soviets saw his work as a 'Western propaganda campaign'.

For the UN Secretary-General, Van Boven's speech was the last straw; he bowed to growing pressure from a number of governments and dismissed him.

The background to the sacking of Theo van Boven illustrates a number of important points about the United Nations as an organisation for promoting human rights. First, it is made up of independent states which are, above all else, concerned to protect their own interests and those of their allies. Many of its commissions and committees are, likewise, made up of state representatives who are there, first and foremost, to look after their own country's interests. Second, it is dogged by all the feuds and tensions affecting international affairs. Third, in the final analysis it can only achieve what its member states wish it to achieve or can be manoeuvred into letting it achieve. As a result, a style of 'quiet diplomacy' with respect to human rights questions has had to be evolved. Van Boven's six years of office brought a deviation from that style for which he paid a price.

The United Nations Commission on Human Rights

The Commission on Human Rights was established in 1946 (see Chapter 2). Its first major task was to draft the Universal Declaration of Human Rights. It was also responsible for drawing up the original versions of the two UN Covenants on Human Rights.

Sometimes described as 'the UN's human rights watchdog', it meets for about six weeks each year. In the 1960s the Commission's power was increased so that it was able to deal with human rights in *all* countries. In the late 1960s and early 1970s the Commission investigated human rights in several areas including Southern Africa,

Israeli-occupied Arab territory, Chile, El Salvador, Iran and Poland. In the 1980s the Commission also began to undertake research into various issues such as disappearances, slavery and treatment of indigenous peoples.

How effective is the Commission on Human Rights?

The Secretary-General's office receives between 20,000 and 30,000 complaints about human rights violations each year. How successful is the Human Rights Commission in handling these complaints and in bringing about some change in the behaviour of governments violating human rights?

Clearly, some success has been achieved. The machinery enabling the Commission to set up working or fact-finding groups to investigate consistent patterns of rights violations has been effective in bringing human rights issues to world-wide notice. Reports from the groups are examined by the Commission in public session and receive widespread media coverage. The evidence gathered has been used as a basis for resolutions adopted by the General Assembly. The reports are very detailed despite the fact that only one country investigated (Chile) has permitted the fact-finding group to enter its territory. Governments find it deeply embarrassing when the finger is pointed at them by so prestigious an organisation as the United Nations.

The root problem is that the Commission is caught up in international politics and mirrors the tensions that exist between East and West, North and South. It is made up of representatives who act upon instructions from their own governments. As a result, commitment to human rights is sometimes very much a secondary consideration when a vote is taken. This has led to the Commission condemning relatively minor rights violations whilst sometimes overlooking horrendous violations. For example, the Cambodian regime, 1975–9, pursued a policy of mass executions but escaped condemnation because non-aligned states were reluctant to criticise one of their own members.

When accused by the Commission of human rights violations, governments have two ready-made lines of defence. The first is to claim that the Commission is breaking part of its Charter which prevents UN intervention in the domestic affairs of a member state. The second is to point out that all parties at the UN recognise that rights may have to be suspended in time of crisis or war. Governments often justify their denial of rights by claiming exceptional circumstances at home.

It is easy to become cynical about the Commission's performance. To do so is perhaps to overlook the progress that has been made towards 'giving teeth' to its machinery. The Commission has been described by one expert as having had a 'No Action' doctrine between 1947 and 1967. Since then there has been a slow and rather stealthy accumulation of power and influence. The Commission has no powers to *enforce* observations of human rights. It has to rely on persuasion and world opinion to give effect to any resolutions agreed. Its primary function is therefore as a public platform for embarrassing governments who infringe human rights.

The two International Covenants in action

How effective are the two UN International Covenants, described in Chapter 2? The report machinery set up under the Covenant on Economic, Social and Cultural Rights only began operation in 1980 and immediately ran into difficulties. The Human Rights Committee set up by the Covenant on Civil and Political Rights has fared rather better. Reports from over seventy countries have been examined. On the other hand, the Committee has not considered any inter-state complaints largely because fewer than twenty countries have recognised it as a competent body for doing so.

Only about thirty countries have accepted that the Committee can hear individual complaints filed by their citizens. When the Committee receives a complaint from an individual who has done everything possible to obtain redress in his or her own country, the government concerned is given six months to submit evidence before the case is examined to decide whether or not a rights violation has occurred. The Committee's 'views' are summarised in a UN press release and are also included in its annual report to the General Assembly.

How effective is the Human Rights Committee? One weakness is that its area of concern is restricted to those states that have signed the Covenant on Civil and Political Rights and it is often those countries with a poor rights record who hold back from signing. The number of countries that have ratified the Covenant (seventy or so) is increasing at the rate of four or five per year but, nonetheless, over half the countries of the world have still to sign.

The individual complaints machinery also has weaknesses. Perhaps the greatest is that people are not aware that they *can* complain to the Committee. Between March 1976 and June 1982 the Committee received a mere 116 complaints and these came from citizens of only thirteen of the twenty-seven states that had by then accepted the right to individual petition. The Committee, like much of the UN machinery, works slowly. It normally takes between two and three years to deal with a case from the moment the complaint is received. There is also the question whether the Committee should do more than publish its 'views'. Some members feel they can do no more; others say they should insist on a report from the country concerned describing what action has been taken in the light of the Committee's 'views'.

9 The European Convention: a regional human rights treaty in operation

Mrs Cosans and Mrs Campbell go to court

The cemetery was out of bounds but fifteen-year-old Jeffrey Cosans tried to take a short cut through it on his way home from school. Shortly afterwards he was told to report for punishment to the Assistant Headteacher. The punishment was to take a form that had been common in Scottish schools – blows administered to the palms of the hand by a 'tawse' (leather strap). When Jeffrey reported to the Assistant Headteacher he followed his father's advice and refused to accept corporal punishment. He was immediately suspended and told that he would not be permitted back into school until he was willing to take his punishment. Subsequently the local education authority told Jeffrey's parents that they were prepared to lift the suspension as long as Jeffrey agreed to obey the rules and disciplinary requirements of the school. For their part, Mr and Mrs Cosans insisted that they would not allow their son back into the school unless they received a guarantee that he would not be beaten for any misbehaviour. The deadlock remained unbroken and Jeffrey never returned to school.

Gordon Campbell attended a Roman Catholic primary school in Scotland where the 'tawse' was also used for disciplinary purposes. Gordon had not been given the 'tawse' but his parents, who were opposed in principle to corporal punishment, requested an assurance from the regional council that their son would never be beaten. The council refused to give such a guarantee.

Independently of each other, Mrs Cosans and Mrs Campbell decided to test whether their parental rights, as protected under the European Convention on Human Rights, had been infringed.

In Chapter 2 we saw how the Universal Declaration of Human Rights was adopted in 1948 in the hope of achieving lasting peace by protecting the individual from oppression. The Declaration set a global standard of behaviour for countries to live up to; it did not, and could not, establish the means whereby those standards could be enforced. The nations of Western Europe, many of which had been devastated during the Second World War, saw the need to establish some form of regional machinery for the enforcement of human rights. A first important step was taken in May 1949 when the *Council of Europe* was founded. It was the first European political institution. One of the Council's principal aims was to work for 'the maintenance and further realisation of human rights and fundamental freedoms'. No sooner was it established than it began work preparing a convention – a legally binding international treaty – for the protection of human rights. The hope and expectation was that such a contract among states would have every chance of being effective because the states involved were all packed into one, relatively small, region of the world and because they all shared certain common legal, cultural and political characteristics.

On 4 November 1950, ministers of the fifteen member countries of the Council of Europe met in Rome and signed the *European Convention on Human Rights*. It came into force on 3 September 1953. From then on the legal machinery it set up began to act upon complaints by one member state against another. From 1955 it has also been able to take up complaints from individuals. Not every member state has recognised the right of individual petition.

How does the Convention actually go about protecting human rights in practice? Let us take the sample cases of the Cosans and Campbell families. When Mrs Cosans and Mrs Campbell made their complaints, they were first considered by the *European Commission of Human Rights* which is made up of legal experts elected for six years by the Council of Europe's decision-making body, the Committee of Ministers.

At its meeting in December 1977, the Commission reviewed the claims made by Mrs Cosans and Mrs Campbell that the use of corporal punishment was contrary to Article 3 of the Convention ('no one shall be subjected to torture or to inhuman or degrading treatment or punishment') and also that the mothers' rights under Article 2 of the first Protocol ('the State shall respect the right of parents to ensure education and teaching in conformity with their own religious and philosophical convictions') had been infringed. For their claims to be declared 'admissible', Mrs Cosans and Mrs Campbell had to show that they had tried every possible way of obtaining a remedy for their grievances in their own country. The Commission also had to be satisfied that no more than six months had passed since a final decision had been made on the issue in question by the relevant national court or authority.

The Commission then spent five months establishing the facts surrounding the two cases – looking at Scottish law on corporal punishment, conducting on-the-spot investigations, and gathering written and spoken evidence. It also tried to achieve a friendly settlement between the parties at odds with each other. All its efforts

European Court at Strasbourg in operation.

failed and, so, in May 1980 the Commission delivered a confidential report on the two cases to the Committee of Ministers and to the British government. The report concluded that Article 3 of the Convention had not been infringed (presumably because neither Jeffrey Cosans nor Gordon Campbell had actually been beaten) but that Article 2 of the first Protocol had been violated.

At hearings in September 1981 and January 1982, the Cosans and Campbell cases were considered before the *European Court of Human Rights*. The Court is made up of eminent judges or legal experts who are elected for nine years by the Parliamentary Assembly of the Council of Europe.

Mrs Cosans' and Mrs Campbell's complaints were examined, as is usual, by a panel of seven judges, who followed their normal practice of hearing evidence in public but conducting their discussions in private. They found that 'no violation of Article 3 is established'. Neither Jeffrey Cosans nor Gordon Campbell had been strapped, so the Court was not considering cases in which corporal punishment had actually been inflicted. The judges pointed out, however, that to threaten with torture or degrading punishment might in some circumstances itself be classified as 'inhuman treatment'. They said that Jeffrey 'may well have experienced feelings of apprehension or disquiet' when he came close to being punished with the tawse but such feelings were 'not sufficient to amount to degrading treatment, within the meaning of Article 3'.

The complaint of Mrs Cosans and Mrs Campbell under Article 2 of the first Protocol – which lays down the right of parents to have their children educated and taught in line with their own convictions – caused much discussion at the Court. Both mothers complained that their rights under the article were violated by the use of corporal punishment for disciplinary purposes in the schools attended by their children. The British government disagreed. In its evidence, it argued that discipline was not part of 'education' and 'teaching' but an aspect of 'school administration'. Its obligation to respect the philosophical convictions of parents, it claimed, only applied

Mrs Campbell in February 1982, the day after the European Court ruled in favour of Mrs Cosans and herself.

to lesson content and teaching, and not to other aspects of schooling of which school administration was one. It also pleaded that it had respected the applicants' convictions by adopting a policy of gradually phasing out corporal punishment in Scottish schools. A careful balance had to be struck between the opinions of supporters and opponents of corporal punishment.

The European Court rejected each of the government's arguments. Education, it held, was 'the whole process whereby, in any society, adults endeavour to transmit their beliefs, culture and other values to the young.' The school's disciplinary system was part of that process. The government's duty to respect parental opinion in education (of which discipline is part) could not be set aside because of the need to strike a balance between the conflicting views of parents about the use of the tawse. Mrs Cosans and Mrs Campbell were, therefore, declared by six votes to one to be victims of a human rights violation under Article 2 of the first Protocol.

The European Court's judgement was made public in February 1982. It was described by the teachers' newspaper, *The Times Educational Supplement*, as 'another welcome milestone along the road to the ending of corporal punishment'.

The Cosans and Campbell cases illustrate the intricacies of human rights questions when we descend from considering lofty ideals to implementing and enforcing those ideals. The European Court's judgement was clearly unwelcome to the many parents in favour of corporal punishment. How, then, could the British government act upon the binding judgement of the Court without taking away those parents' rights to an education for *their* children in line with *their* own convictions? One possible answer was to set up 'caning' and 'non-caning' schools and to encourage parents to send their children to the school of their choice. This was seen as both expensive and impracticable as it would have required the building of new schools or long-distance travel for some pupils. Another answer was to set up 'caning' and 'non-caning' classes in the same school. A third was to establish a system whereby parents would have the right to exempt their children from corporal punishment.

The British government responded to the Court's judgement in August 1983 by opting for the third alternative. A 'consultation document' was published rejecting a total ban on corporal punishment but saying that it was the government's intention to pass a law allowing parents to contract their children out of being beaten at school.

The government's decision was condemned on many sides as likely to create a sense of injustice amongst pupils and parents: 'As soon as parents see that little Gavin is being beaten and little Johnny is not for the same offence, they will see the system is totally unjust and condemn it.' Put another way, government endeavours to promote and protect the *individual liberties* of parents were likely to fall foul of the need for *equality*.

Eventually, the British parliament passed an amendment to the 1986 Education Bill, outlawing corporal punishment. From August 1987, teachers who beat, tawse, cane or slap pupils in state-supported schools are liable to civil actions for battery.

The European Convention: an assessment

By 1 January 1982 only seventy-four cases had been heard before the Court. They covered a wide range of issues. In 1978, for example, the court found the British government had contravened Article 3 of the Convention by allowing soldiers to use certain interrogation techniques against prisoners during the Northern Ireland emergency of 1971. These techniques were hooding, use of electronic noises, making prisoners stand for long periods with fingers pressed against a wall, deprivation of sleep and a bread-and-water diet. The British government was cleared of torture but was judged to have permitted practices which amounted to 'inhuman and degrading' treatment. The complaint to the Commission had been put by the government of the Republic of Ireland. The Court has also dealt with cases concerning restrictions on prisoners' rights of correspondence, the use of the birch in the Isle of Man, the status of illegitimate children in Belgium,

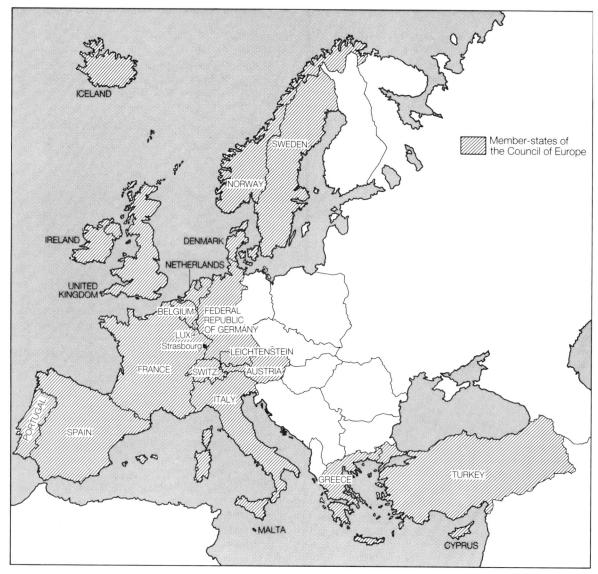

wire-tapping in West Germany, compulsory sex education in schools and the rights of mentally-subnormal offenders to have their detention reviewed.

How successful and effective is the European Convention on Human Rights? What are its strengths and weaknesses? What broader issues are raised by its work and its very existence?

Let us look at two of its principal weaknesses. Firstly, the Convention affords no protection to social and economic rights. To fill this gap a *European Social Charter* was launched in 1961 and came into force in 1963. The Charter sets out nineteen rights and principles which states *can* accept as aims of their social and economic policy (for example, the right to work, the right to strike, the right to social security). States signing the Charter pick and choose which bits to accept. The Charter has no effective complaints or enforcement machinery.

A second criticism often made of the Convention's machinery is that it is very slow and cumbersome in dealing with complaints. The incidents which triggered off the Cosans and Campbell cases occurred in 1976; the Court's judgement was given in 1982. It is this time-lag between complaints and judgements which is causing some concern at the Commission.

On the other hand it could be argued that the time taken over cases is one of the real strengths of the Convention's machinery. The European Commission and Court are not in the business of punishing wrongdoers; their relationship with member states is not that of prosecuter and accused. Governments are not found 'guilty' or 'punished'. If a human right has been violated, the Commission never approaches the government concerned as though it had wilfully violated that right. As it sees it, violations happen because of an oversight on the government's part, because of outdated law or because of a misinterpretation of the Convention. The Commission's role is, therefore, one of working in co-operation with member states to eliminate infringements of the Convention. The ultimate aim is to harmonise the letter and practice of the law between member states. Co-operation to this end would have been less easy to achieve save for the painstaking consultations that take place behind the scenes between the Commission and the government concerned over each complaint, the Commission's policy of limiting their examination of each case before them to the strict facts so as not to raise too many issues at once and the confidential nature of much of the Commission's work. Each court finding against a member state could be construed as undermining the state's sovereignty. That only one state has openly clashed with the Commission (Greece under a military regime, 1967–74) speaks oceans for its slow, confidence-building way of achieving change. The Convention and its machinery also have an *educative* role; as more and more issues are raised and as further judgements of the Strasbourg Court see the light of day, the people of Western Europe are undoubtedly becoming more conscious of human rights.

The other major strength of the European Convention is that it applies to a fairly tightly knit region of the world. The geographical area covered by the Convention is comparatively small and the countries in question possess many similarities. In consequence, the Convention has proved effective and is a model which is beginning to be copied in the Americas, Africa, the Caribbean and Asia.

10 Amnesty International and other pressure groups

Amnesty International

In 1975, Julio de Pena Valdez, a trade union leader in the Dominican Republic, was seized by the police and held naked in a prison cell. His case came to the notice of Amnesty International. Amnesty carried out an investigation and, satisfied that a human rights violation had taken place, urged its members world-wide to write letters and Christmas cards on his behalf. Early in 1976 Julio de Pena Valdez was released on the direct command of the Dominican President. Later, he described the effect of the Amnesty campaign for his release:

> When the first two hundred letters came, the guards gave me back my clothes. Then the next two hundred letters came and the prison director came to see me. When the next pile of letters arrived, the director got in touch with his superior. The letters kept coming and coming: three thousand of them. The President was informed. The letters still kept arriving and the President called the prison and told them to let me go.
> After I was released the President called me to his office for a man-to-man talk. He said: 'How is it that a trade union leader like you has so many friends all over the world?' He showed me an enormous box full of letters he had received and, when we parted, he gave them to me. I still have them.

Julio's story is, in many respects, a typical example of Amnesty International in action. Amnesty was founded in 1961 by Peter Benenson, a Catholic lawyer of Jewish descent who had English and Russian parents. Benenson hit upon the idea of working for the release of 'prisoners of conscience' (people imprisoned for their beliefs) by means of letter-writing campaigns.

By the close of 1961, Amnesty International groups had been established in twelve countries (ten Western European countries plus Australia and the United States). Benenson had also chosen the symbol by which Amnesty is now recognised throughout the world – the candle in barbed wire. Benenson's choice of symbol had been inspired by the Chinese proverb, 'Better to light one candle than to curse the darkness'.

Today, Amnesty has over 250,000 members in some 140 countries. There are more than 2,500 groups 'adopting' prisoners of conscience. The International Secretariat, based in London, numbers 150 employees, nearly half of whom are involved in researching the details of human rights violations. As was the case in 1961, Amnesty groups are strongest and most active in Western Europe.

Amnesty's aims and techniques have changed very little since its inception. Its fundamental concern is to achieve the immediate and

Peter Benenson, founder of Amnesty International.

unconditional release of prisoners of conscience *provided they have never used or advocated violence*. It also works to ensure that political prisoners are given a fair and prompt trial. Its third aim is to seek the abolition of the death penalty and the elimination of the use of torture and inhuman and degrading punishments on *all* prisoners.

When Amnesty learns of an arrest or case of imprisonment where there appears to have been a violation of basic human rights, the Research Department in London goes into action to check out the details of the case and to establish whether the person should be 'adopted' as a prisoner of conscience. Amnesty would not adopt the prisoner if he or she had used or condoned violence. (This is why the black South African leader, Nelson Mandela, was dropped as a prisoner of conscience in 1964 after he had been convicted of sabotage). A dossier on the prisoner is compiled which is passed on to local Amnesty groups once the prisoner is adopted.

The 'adoption group' has been described as 'the central cog' in Amnesty's machinery. Some are attached to churches, others to schools, colleges and universities, others to factories and places of work. Yet again, an adoption group might be based on a neighbourhood and have no affiliation to a particular local institution. The group writes letters to the prisoners they are asked to adopt, to their jailers, to the governments and embassies concerned and to newspapers. Sometimes the group might mount a petition or organise a public protest in support of a particular prisoner; occasionally they might raise money to help a prisoner's family or to pay for a defence lawyer.

Examples of Amnesty letters sent to prisoners of conscience.

Excellence,

Je suis très désolé à cause du destin de ▓▓▓▓▓, qui, sans avoir violé la loi de votre pays, est emprisonné depuis 1976 sans jugement dans les „camps d'internement administratifs", en dernier lieu à Tchollire. Je sais que son état de santé est très mauvais! Je vous pri instamment de libérer tout de suite Monsieur Gaspard Mouen.

Avec l'expression de ma haute considération.

Exzellenz,

Ich bin sehr betroffen über das Schicksal von ▓▓▓▓▓, der, ohne Gerichtsurteil in „administrativen Internierungslagern", zuletzt in Tchollire, in Haft ist.

Ich weiß, sein Gesundheitszustand ist sehr schlecht!

Ich bitte Sie dringend um sofortige Freilassung von Herrn Gaspard Mouen.

Hochachtungsvoll

Your Excellency

I respectfully urge you to ensure the physical safety of ▓▓▓▓▓ who, according to reports, is seriously ill and in need of medical treatment after being tortured on at least four separate occasions. As he is regarded as a prisoner of conscience he should be released immediately.

Yours respectfully and sincerely

SIT DOWN AND WRITE

An Amnesty International poster.

Such labour requires a very high level of dedication on the part of those involved. Save in rare cases the group will never hear directly from the adopted prisoner and, even if released, they can never be sure whether their work really helped in any way. Set against this lack of direct 'feedback' are Amnesty estimates that between five and six prisoners are released each day as a result of letter-writing campaigns. Governments of all persuasions are clearly embarrassed by the glare of publicity they receive when a prisoner in their hands is adopted by Amnesty.

Another method employed by Amnesty to combat human rights violations is its Urgent Action Scheme. This involves a world-wide network of members of the public who send (and pay for) telegrams and letters on behalf of individuals whose cases need immediate action. Urgent Action is often used when a person disappears in a country where disappearance has come to mean torture or summary execution. It is used, too, in cases where people are being sent back to their country of origin from which they fled for political reasons. It is also used in an effort to stop death penalties being carried out. The scheme works through national Urgent Action Co-ordinators who send out case sheets. Scheme members are expected to send off a letter or telegram within forty-eight hours of receipt of a sheet. In 1980, Amnesty launched some 295 Urgent Actions; the organisation estimates that the condition of the prisoner is improved in over forty per cent of cases taken up.

Amnesty also uses the special mission as an important tool in its campaigning work. In its first twenty years over 350 missions went to different countries. Most are sent to carry out investigations into human rights denials. Some, however, are sent to observe public trials whilst others are sent as delegations to governments with the task of putting Amnesty's viewpoint on some aspect of government policy or practice. The reports compiled and published as a result of investigative missions are usually given considerable press coverage and this has helped to dramatise human rights issues before the public eye.

Raising public consciousness on human rights questions is also a major aim of the special campaigns launched from time to time by Amnesty. In the 1970s and early 1980s torture was the subject of an ongoing campaign, the 1973 *Report on Torture* containing horrific evidence of the need for world-wide action to stamp out its use. In 1978 Amnesty ran a special campaign to highlight cruelty to children carried out as a means of punishing or silencing their parents. The year before, a special effort had been made to enlist trade union support for its work. As a result, the British Trades Union Congress of 1977 passed a resolution urging support for Amnesty's work 'on behalf of trade unionists who are detained or subject to torture for their activities'.

What are the strengths of Amnesty's approach? What are its weaknesses?

On the 'plus' side is the highly respected quality of Amnesty's research which means that any decision to adopt, undertake Urgent Action or send a mission is based upon a meticulously compiled system of facts. Another great asset is the depth of volunteer support upon which Amnesty can rely for its postal campaigns which are based upon a simple but, it seems, proven faith in the power of the pen. Amnesty's policy of limiting itself to defending just a few certain basic rights also enables it to be a remarkably efficient and effective pressure group. Finally, its insistence upon appearing impartial gains it much respect. To ensure that adoption groups appear politically neutral, they are asked to adopt more than one prisoner at a time. The prisoners will never be from the same type of political system, but each from states that differ politically (e.g. one Communist, one Western, one non-aligned). In addition, groups are not allowed to work for prisoners of their own country.

On the 'minus' side is the fact that Amnesty by and large remains a pressure group based in the Capitalist countries of the 'rich north'. This brings us to a further criticism made of Amnesty; that what some see as its strength – its deliberate policy of limiting its concern to certain basic rights – is in fact a weakness in that it overlooks violations of security-oriented rights – so vital to the poor. Amnesty responds by saying that different categories of rights cannot be separated and that its defence of some rights helps towards the protection of other rights. If people's voices are not stilled by imprisonment, it will be easier to achieve food, clothing, shelter and other basic needs for all.

The Anti-Slavery Society

The Anti-Slavery Society for the Protection of Human Rights is the world's oldest human rights organisation. Founded in 1839 the society works to end all forms of slavery and to defend the rights of indigenous peoples; it also endeavours to protect the rights of those who are 'vulnerable to oppression or exploitation on account of their hunger, poverty... or social, geographical or political isolation'. When satisfied that human rights violations have taken place, a report is sent to the government concerned for investigation and comment. Depending upon the reply received, the Society decides whether to work

Debt-bondage in Bahir, India, 1984. As bonded labourers these women no longer have control over their lives and cannot sell their labour on the free market. Their husbands, in debt to the landowner for however small a sum, find themselves trapped in a life-long struggle to repay the burden of debt and interest, and may be forced into letting themselves, their wives and their children work for nothing.

SURVIVAL INTERNATIONAL
FOR THE RIGHTS OF THREATENED TRIBAL PEOPLES

'First they came for the Jews
and I did not speak out –
because I was not a Jew.

Then they came for the communists
and I did not speak out –
because I was not a communist.

Then they came for the trade
unionists and I did not speak out –
because I was not a trade unionist.

Then they came for me –
and there was no one left
to speak out for me.'

Poem by Pastor Niemoeller,
prominent in Church resistance to
the Nazis.

BLACK OR WHITE?

A Minority Rights Group poster.

quietly 'behind the scenes' to achieve change or to 'go public' about the case. Recent activities (jointly with Survival International) have included the intervention in 1974 to free the Andoke, an Amazonian Indian tribe from Colombia of 120 persons, from debt bondage to a rubber merchant. Since 1981 the Anti-Slavery Society has mounted a campaign against the exploitation of tribal peoples by the Philippine government and by transnational companies working on behalf of the government. Tribal homelands had been invaded and industrial and energy schemes started without consultation or agreement.

The Minority Rights Group

The Minority Rights Group concerns itself with oppressed minorities – and majorities – whether indigenous or non-indigenous. Its main method is to publish reports on peoples suffering prejudice, discrimination and oppression. Over seventy reports have been published on peoples such as the Tamils of Sri Lanka, the Untouchables of India and Haitian refugees in the United States. The reports have been very influential in promoting world-wide concern about the treatment of minorities and new reports receive good press coverage in newspapers around the world. The Minority Rights Group also runs an educational programme in schools and colleges, teaching about human rights and minority groups, and counteracting bias and stereotypes. The organisation was awarded the United Nations Association Media Peace Prize for 1982.

The work of such groups as the Anti-Slavery Society, Survival International and the Minority Rights Group is all the more important in that the peoples they try to protect more often than not have a very limited chance of influencing those in power. They tend to have too few votes or too little political 'muscle' to be able to make themselves heard. Likewise, there is usually no political or interest group in the country concerned which sees itself as profiting by helping them. They also provide a convenient scapegoat should the government fall on difficult times. The task, therefore, often falls on organisations outside the country in question to defend the rights of an oppressed indigenous or minority group. It is an indication of the poor track record of the United Nations in defending minorities that much of the job still has to be done by non-governmental pressure groups.

Organisations combating Apartheid

Two organisations concerned with promoting the rights of an oppressed *majority* are the Anti-Apartheid Movement and the International Defence and Aid Fund for Southern Africa (IDAF). Both organisations work for the liberation of the black peoples of South Africa who are denied the right to full and equal participation in political, social and economic life by a white minority which numbers only 20 per cent of the population.

Campaign Against the Arms Trade

The work of the Campaign Against Arms Trade (CAAT) straddles all categories of human rights. CAAT works towards an end in the trade in arms and seeks socially useful alternatives to arms manufacture. The organisation argues that governments are spending huge sums of money on the purchase of arms when that money could be used to promote the welfare of all. CAAT particularly criticises the governments who *sell* arms, actively encouraging their purchase through arms sales fairs. The best customers of the major arms-exporting nations are often notorious for human rights violations, and the arms may be used not only for defence against external aggression but for maintaining control against internal opposition as well. In the last few years, CAAT has also called for an export ban on devices which can be – and are being – used for prison control and torture. In 1982, for instance, a campaign was mounted against the export of pocket electric shock prods which were on offer at the June British Army Equipment Exhibition, a sales exercise to which representatives of many foreign governments were invited.

British Council of Churches

Another important human rights body is the British Council of Churches (BCC), an 'Associated Member' of the World Council of Churches. BCC has established an Advisory Forum on Human Rights which publishes literature explaining the Christian standpoint on human rights and giving case studies of rights violations world-wide. BCC has also established a Community and Race Relations Unit to combat racism in British society.

British Council of Churches leaflet.

'The world is moving in two directions: one is towards the narrowing of distances through travel, increasing interchange between scientists (who take a world view of problems such as the exploitation of space, ecology, population): the other is towards the shutting down of frontiers, the ever more jealous surveillance by governments and police of individual freedom. The opposites are fear and openness; and in being concerned with the situation of those who are deprived of their freedoms one is taking the side of openness.'
Stephen Spender, *trustee of WSET*

The Writers and Scholars Educational Trust

The Writers and Scholars Educational Trust (WSET) is a registered UK charity which aims to promote freedom of expression and information and which opposes censorship world-wide. WSET publishes the magazine *Index on Censorship*, which appears ten times a year and contains case studies of repression of information and examples of censored material. It has also arranged exhibitions of banned art and lectures by writers whose work has been banned.

A poster for *Index on Censorship*.

Organisations promoting human rights in the United States

Indian Law Resource Center

The Center plays a leading part in the effort to protect and develop the rights of Indian people throughout North, Central and South America. While Indian cultures, languages and religions have survived, Indian people have practically no legally-protectable right to maintain their heritage, nor to stop government confiscation of their lands and property: in some countries, Indians are being imprisoned, displaced and killed on a vast scale. The Center, an Indian-controlled organisation, gives legal support to Indian nations and communities, and fights to change existing law which often condemns Indians to deplorable living conditions on Indian reserves. Their work includes challenging discriminatory laws in the United States, recovering and protecting Indian land, and recently supporting the Alaskan natives in their fight to preserve their lands and subsistence economies.

Humanitas International

Founded by singer and peace campaigner Joan Baez, Humanitas works for the protection of human rights world-wide. The preservation of human life and human dignity are its highest priorities. The organisation carries out research, educates the public on human rights issues and provides emergency relief to refugees. Humanitas has consistently spoken out against, for example, disappearances in Latin America and the harassment of Soviet dissidents.

Helsinki Watch (USA)

Helsinki Watch focuses on human rights in the thirty-five countries in Eastern and Western Europe and North America which signed the 1975 Helsinki agreement on security and co-operation in Europe (see Chapter 2). It publicises violations of human rights, encourages international protests against offending governments and organises public and private meetings.

Human Rights in Australia

The Human Rights Commission is a body which promotes and protects human rights in Australia. Set up by the Commonwealth government in 1981, it investigates complaints, reviews legislation, and undertakes educational programmes dealing with human rights, as well as ensuring that the Racial Discrimination Act (1975) and the Sex Discrimination Act (1984) are effectively implemented. People who feel that their rights are being violated can complain to the Commission, who will then look into the complaint and take the necessary action.

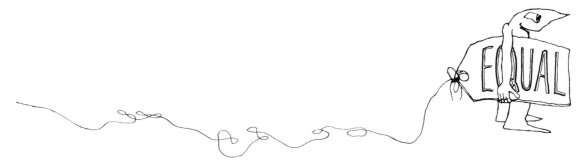

11   Individuals and human rights

Students attending a school in a run-down inner-city quarter of Newark in the north-eastern United States were becoming increasingly concerned. Their school was in what officials called a 'declining area'; there were flats, houses and tenement blocks ready for demolition, the streets were often unpaved and generally poorly lit. The students wanted to do something so they invited community leaders into school to advise them. The advice was sound. 'Don't try and change all that's wrong with your community,' they were told. 'Pick a specific issue and concentrate on that.' They chose the poor street-lighting. There had been a bad accident recently at a spot where there were few lights and, even more recently, a girl had been raped in one badly lit street. The class spent a lot of time preparing a petition and asking people in the neighbourhood to sign it. Eventually they put their case and presented their petition at a City of Newark Public Hearing. As a result of their work, the Newark Council debated the street-lighting problem but little action followed. They nonetheless had the satisfaction of knowing that they had raised public consciousness about an important local issue. Students at a school in Bedford-Stuyvesent, a poor inner-city quarter of New York, were spectacularly successful in their campaign to combat famine in Ethiopia. In little over three weeks, helped by a US Congressman, they raised over half a million dollars by putting on dance and drama performances, by giving up sweets, or candy, and by encouraging other schools to become involved in fund-raising ventures. The students bought wheat, chartered a cargo aircraft and had it flown to Addis Ababa, from where the wheat was transported by truck to the relief camps. Meanwhile their teachers taught them about the political and economic causes of the Ethiopian famine, 'Don't ever tell me again that "you can't do something about it",' declared one of the students after the successful conclusion of the campaign.

In a Midlands school in England a group of girls decided to test whether the local city had adequate facilities for disabled people. They hired a wheelchair and wheeled one of their number into shops, cafés, restaurants, banks and offices. They also took the wheelchair on local buses. Following their experience, they wrote a critical report about facilities for the disabled, copies of which were sent to relevant local bodies.

In the same school students run a Tools for Self-Reliance group. They spend time over lunch and after school collecting old and disused tools from people in the neighbourhood, cleaning and preparing them in the school workshops, and packaging them for eventual transportation to villages in Tanzania. Some other students give time over to writing letters to and on behalf of political prisoners adopted by Amnesty International. During the May 1979 General Election yet another group of students attended constituency meetings and questioned candidates on human rights and other world issues.

All the activities described above are examples of young people

Volunteers refurbishing tools in the school workshop.

Tools supplied by 'Tools for Self Reliance' in use by craftsmen near Bulawayo, Zimbabwe. Collecting and refurbishing old and unwanted tools is a practical way of giving support.

showing an active concern in one way or another for human rights. Such examples show that individuals and, especially, groups of individuals working together are not powerless. Confronted by a world of so many huge problems, it is tempting to bury our heads, ostrich-like, in the sand. The very immensity of the problems we face encourages such a response. Yet there is plenty of evidence demonstrating that we, as individuals, can alter the world in which we find ourselves. *Learning about* human rights is, ultimately, not enough; if our aim is to be able to protect our human rights and also defend the human rights of others, then we need *practice*. As the students described above found out, school can provide an excellent arena and springboard for such practice.

How do we 'get involved'? Broadly speaking, there are three ways: first, by achieving publicity for human rights questions so that people know what is going on, and what the issues are; second, by trying to influence the decision-makers at local, national and international level; third, by joining organisations and participating in their work.

Bringing human rights questions to public notice is not as difficult as it first seems for there are so many outlets for publicity. Students can write letters to newspapers and magazines, local and national: there are school magazines, church magazines, community newsletters, local trade papers, and many magazines for young people have letter columns. Radio outlets should be explored too. National and local radio stations have phone-ins for people to put their views on matters of concern to them. Many disc jockeys are more than happy, too, to air subjects of concern to young people. Another idea is to organise letter campaigns to radio and television stations urging that they give more air time to human rights questions.

There are many ways, too, of achieving publicity by putting on displays, exhibitions and drama. At one school, a group of students prepared an exhibition on Apartheid in South Africa and then took the exhibition to church halls and schools in the area. At another school, a group publicised human rights themes by putting on street theatre in the local market and shopping centre. At a third school, a 'Rock against Racism' concert replaced the school's annual Gilbert and Sullivan operetta.

A group from Stokesley School in North Yorkshire lobbies parliament.

Nor is it that difficult to try and influence those who make the decisions about our lives. Anyone can write to or petition their political representatives – their local MP, or their Congressman or woman and Senator (in the USA), so that the matter may be pursued at a higher level. Such representatives rarely disregard issues that are exciting the concern of their constituents. The more letters on an issue, the more the political parties will take note. Nor should letters and petitions to businesses and other organisations be discounted. Students could, for instance, petition a local branch of a transnational company that is reported to be grossly underpaying its employees in the Third World. They might, on another occasion, write to a trade union branch that has behaved in a racist or sexist manner.

There are also many organisations involved in the business of promoting and protecting human rights and many of these welcome voluntary help. Some are involved in fund and consciousness-raising for the world-wide fight against disease, hunger and poverty; some are principally concerned with protecting liberty-oriented rights; others campaign on a specific platform (e.g. against Apartheid, censorship, slavery, torture). Many have – or are ready to support the establishment of – local branches.

Extracts from the Students' Rights and Responsibilities Manual observed in all public high schools in the San Francisco Unified School District.

8 Students have the right to democratic representation in administrative committees affecting students and student rights.

9 Students have the right to participate in the development of rules and regulations to which they are subject and the right to be notified of such rules and regulations.

10 Legal guardians or authorized representatives, or students if authorized, have the right to see their own student's personal files...etc., at anytime during school hours and have the right to be notified if adverse comments are placed in such records.

12 Students on their own school campus may exercise their constitutionally protected rights of free speech and assembly so long as they do not interfere with the regular school program

(a) Students have the right to wear political buttons, armbands, or any other badges of symbolic expression.

(b) Students have the right to form political and social organizations.

(c) Students have the right to use bulletin boards without prior censorship requirement or approval.

(f) Students have the right to determine their own appearance, including the style of their hair and clothing.

School students may also be concerned about their own rights! As we have seen, the rights we claim can never be exercised in an unrestricted way but some would argue that students' rights are often excessively and unnecessarily curtailed in schools that claim to be breeding grounds for democracy and responsibility. To what extent, for instance, do schools permit freedom of expression and give students an effective voice in decision-making processes (such as student notice board space, a school council with real power, a student-controlled newsletter)? To what extent is student freedom of association (e.g the right to form organisations, the right to space and facilities for student meetings) respected? To what extent do students – and their parents – have access to information recorded about them in school files? Do they have the right to challenge and correct such information?

Then again, we would need to decide how the rights of students in relation to their school might be determined. To what extent should student rights be limited by age considerations? Against the rights of which other interested parties would the rights claimed by students have to be balanced and, hence, limited (e.g. teachers, parents, caretaking and canteen staff, governors)? Do student obligations to their parents and to the state – which offers them a free education – place limitations on their free exercise of rights? Does the law of the land restrict the rights students might claim as morally theirs? What machinery would be needed to protect students' rights and to give students a means of redress should they consider their agreed rights to have been violated?

It is a challenging and important exercise to think about the nature of a charter of student rights for the school of which you are a member. The issues raised above demand serious consideration not least because the Universal Declaration lays down that everybody is entitled to an education that strengthens respect for human rights and fundamental freedoms. As the twenty-first century approaches it is ever more vital that schools create a greater consciousness of human rights given the many different threats facing world society. As one writer has put it:

Human rights do not stop at counting political prisoners any more than they stop at counting the unemployed. Human rights are about human needs – needs that extend from proper nutrition, clothing, shelter, healthcare and education to participating in the decisions that frame our lives.

Further resources

Introductory resources

Amnesty International, *Teaching and Learning about Human Rights*, 1983

Coussins, J., *Taking Liberties: An Introduction to Equal Rights*, Virago, 1979

Cunningham, J., *Human Rights and Wrongs*, Writers and Scholars Educational Trust, 1981

Edmunds, J., *Rights, Responsibilities and the Law*, Nelson/ILEA, 1982

Hayes, D., *Human Rights*, Wayland, 1980

Jordanhill Project in International Understanding (c/o Jordanhill College, Glasgow G13 1PP), *Human Rights*, 1980

Levin, L., *Human Rights. Questions and Answers*, UNESCO, 1981

McGregor, I., *Human Rights*, Batsford, 1975

Pettman, R., *Teaching for Human Rights*, Hodja for the Human Rights Commission (Australia), 1984

Rae, M., Hewitt, P. & Hugill, B., *First Rights*, National Council for Civil Liberties, 1981

Richardson, R. (ed.), *Fighting for Freedom*, Nelson, 1977

Royston, R., *Human Rights*, Macdonald, 1978

Woodhouse, S., *Your Life, My Life: Introduction to Human Rights and Responsibilities*, Writers and Scholars Educational Trust, 1980

Comment

Twelve-unit pack. Well-illustrated.

Lively pack on equality between the sexes.

Good introductory material on civil and political rights.

Well-illustrated practical book on rights in the UK.

Useful 'starter' text but thin on detail and discussion.
Collection of documents and some class activities.

Helpful introduction to UN's work in human rights with an article by article discussion of the Universal Declaration.

Well-illustrated introduction.
Some useful classroom activities.

Handbook on young people's rights.

Excellent 'starter' for class and group discussion work; highly illustrated.

Short introductory work, attractively illustrated and presented.

Introduction to rights for 10–14 year olds.

Facts and figures

Case Studies of rights denials and violations: write to Amnesty International for its publications list; also to the Minority Rights Group for its list of reports (for the addresses of these and other human rights organisations, see page 79).

Comparative study of degrees of freedom in different societies: Humana, C., *World Human Rights Guide*, Hutchinson, 1983. Percentage rating of countries based on civil and political rights only.

Comprehensive handbook on British, US and international organisations concerned with rights: Writers and Scholars Educational Trust, *The Human Rights Handbook*, Macmillan, 1979.

Educational organisations working in human rights and related fields: Drake, P., (ed.), *World Studies Resource Guide*, CEWC, 1987. Write to the Council for Education in World Citizenship at Seymour Mews House, Seymour Mews, London W1H 9PE.

Human rights statistics in map form: Kidron, M., and Segal, R., *The New State of World Atlas*, Pan, 1984.

World spending on arms and social/economic development: Sivard, R. L., *World Military and Social Expenditures*, World Priorities, USA, annual. Available in UK from Campaign Against Arms Trade.

Audio-visual resources

The biggest and best UK collection of 16 mm and video films on human rights is held by Concord Films Council, 201 Felixstowe Road, Ipswich, Suffolk IP3 9BJ. Concord publishes a *List of Films on Human Rights*. Films on human rights are also available from the Human Rights Resource Centre, 45 Denning Street, London NW3. For ideas on how to use films on rights and related subjects in class, see Taylor, N., and Richardson, R., *Seeing and Perceiving*, Ikon/Concord Films Council, 1979.

Visiting speakers

A register of speakers prepared to visit schools and talk on rights-related topics is available from the Centre of Global Education, University of York, York YO1 5DD. Entitled *Speaking Out*, it offers advice on using visiting speakers in class and gives details of over 500 speakers.

Human rights organisations

A list of human rights organisations is available from the Centre for Global Education (address above).
If you write to any of the organisations on the list, remember three things: (1) say exactly what you want – do not send vague general requests, (2) enclose a large stamped addressed envelope and (3) preferably, agree to one class member writing a letter on behalf of everybody rather than flooding the organisation with lots of individual requests.

Index